Descendants of Ambrose Edwards

Generation 1

1. **AMBROSE**[1] **EDWARDS** was born on 16 Apr 1805 in Wilkes County, Georgia. He died on 06 Oct 1884 in Dale County, Alabama. He married Emeline James Gaulding, daughter of John Gaulding and Martha Gaulding in 1827 in South Carolina. She was born on 10 Feb 1810 in Virginia. She died on 01 Jan 1886 in Dale County, Alabama.

I0776329

More About Ambrose Edwards:
Burial: Pleasant Hill Methodist Cemetery, Ozark, Alabama
Living In: 1830 Talbot County, Georgia
Living In: 1840   Russell County, Alabama
Occupation: 1850 in Russell County, Alabama; Farmer
Occupation: 1860 in Dale County, Alabama; Farmer
Occupation: 1870 in Dale County, Alabama; Farmer
Occupation: 1880 in Dale County, Alabama; Farmer
Military Service: Matthews Company, Dale County Reserves, Dale County, Alabama C.S.A.
Property: 1850 in Russell County, Alabama; 150 Acres Improved and 252 Acres Unimproved
Property: 1860 in Dale County, Alabama; 260 Acres Improved and 260 Acres Unimproved
Property: 1870 in Dale County, Alabama; 1250 Acres Improved and 500 Acres Unimproved
Property: 1880 in Dale County, Alabama; 75 Acres Improved and 360 Acres Unimproved

Notes for Ambrose Edwards:
Originally buried in Pleasant Hill Cemetery near Westville, moved to new Pleasant Hill Cemetery near Ozark in 1942 when Fort Rucker was established
----
Moved to Talbot County, Georgia in 1829.
Moved to Russell County, Alabama in 1839. This part of Russell County is now in Lee County, Alabama
Moved to Dale County, Alabama near Westville in November 1854.

Obituary of Ambrose Edwards
Crittenden's Mill, Ala. December 7th 1884 (Published in the Southern Star, December 31, 1884)

Ambrose Edwards was born in Wilkes county Georgia, April 16th 1805 and died in Dale county Alabama, October the 6th 1884, in triumphs of the Christian faith. He was happily married to Emeline J. Gaulding October the 4th 1827 in Bibb county Georgia. In 1820 he moved to Talbot county Georgia and in 1839 he settled in Russell county Alabama where he joined the Methodist Episcopal Church and was Happily converted to God in which faith and communion he lived a consistent and devoted member to the date of his death. He was the father of eleven children five of whom have preceded him to the better land and the other six (all sons) are trying to follow in the footsteps of their father: one a minister of the gospel: four are superintendents of Sabbath schools and the other a church secretary.

No wife ever had a more devoted husband, no children a more affectionate father. His greatest ambition in life was to do good and to see his children good and honorable. Of the seven boys he raised to be men not a dram drinker nor a profane swearer was in the number. He was for many years a practical steward of the church till the mantle fell on his oldest son. He was a man of great will power but was always conservative in his intercourse with his fellow man. Few men were ever more instrumental in settling difficulties between brethren and neighbors than he.

While he was deprived of an early education his practical good sence always gave him first rank in the county where he lived. The last thirty years of his life was spent in Dale county. The writer was with him day and night the greater portion of his last sickness: and such patience he hardly ever witnessed. The only thing that seemed to trouble his mind was leaving his aged and devoted companion who had shared his joys and sorrows through a married life of fifty-seven years. What a happy reunion it will be when the companion who still lingers on the shore of time only waiting for the summons, and the children all meet if faithful around the throne of God.

More About Emeline James Gaulding:
Burial: Pleasant Hill Methodist Cemetery, Ozark, Alabama

Notes for Emeline James Gaulding:
Originally buried in Pleasant Hill Cemetery near Westville, moved to new Pleasant Hill Cemetery near Ozark in 1942 when Fort Rucker was established.

Obituary of Emeline James Gaulding

Emeline J. Edwards, daughter of John Gaulding, was born in the state of Virginia in the month of February 1810. With her parents she removed to Hancock County Georgia in 1818. In that County she was converted at the age of eleven years and joined the Methodist E. Church, in which communion she lived sixty-four years without a stain upon her pure and spotless character. During the year 1827 she was married to Mr. Ambrose Edwards of Monroe County, Georgia. A few years after the happy event they removed to Alabama and settled in old Russell County. Although at the time of their marriage Mr. Edwards was not a member of any Church, not a professor in Jesus Christ, yet by her pure and sweet spirit he was so powerfully influenced in regard to salvation from sin and death as to become deeply concerned. At Salem, of old Russell County, 1839 he was converted and joined the Church of his Christian (.......?) In November 1854 they removed to Dale County and settled near Pleasant Hill Church and became members of that Church.

She was the mother of 11 children, 8 sons and 3 daughters, 5 of whom are dead and 6 living. All of those who lived to sufficient age joined the Church of their fond parents and are strong and devoted members of the Church. Such was the influence of the mother upon the whole family that they are perfectly united in affection, religion and cooperation. In this respect they constitute a model family. How ever distant from each other the children realize their unity in the mother. While breathing her last, a present was received, the gift of a son in Texas. As mother and grandmother she was an extraordinary woman. As wife she was all the Bible commands. As Church member and Christian she was perfect. To everybody she was tender, gentle and considerate. She always had a word of cheer and smile of appreciation for the toiling and struggling ones in righteousness. She heartily endorsed every enterprise of her Church and supported it's institution. Her Pastor always found her in sympathy with his efforts to build up the Church and save sinners. The writer has known her 30 years and knows no fault in her life. At 7 A. M. January 1, 1886 she ascended to glory. She died at the home of her son, C.A.B. Edwards, and was buried at Pleasant Hill on Saturday beside her husband, amid tears of sorrow and hope.

By Rev. Angus Dowling

Ambrose Edwards and Emeline James Gaulding had the following children:

2. i. MARTHA LOUISE[2] EDWARDS was born on 20 Jul 1828 in Georgia. She died on 09 Aug 1881 in Alabama. She married Hope Hull Mizell, son of William Mizell and Mary Love on 07 Dec 1843 in Russell County, Alabama. He was born on 20 Sep 1820 in Baldwin County, Georgia. He died on 02 Mar 1887 in Haw Ridge, Alabama.

3. ii. LEROY MARION EDWARDS was born on 29 Aug 1830 in Talbot County, Georgia. He died on 24 May 1898 in Brundidge, Alabama. He married Martha Mizell, daughter of William Mizell and Mary Love on 06 Nov 1849 in Russell County, Alabama. She was born on 04 Feb 1829 in Houston County, Georgia. She died on 30 Oct 1908 in Brundidge, Pike County, Alabama.

iii. JOHN WILSON GAULDING EDWARDS was born on 10 Jan 1833 in Talbot County, Georgia. He died about 1858. He married Sarah Frances Sharp, daughter of Jehu Harrison Sharp and Tabitha Jane White on 04 Oct 1854 in Meriwether County, Georgia. She was born on 30 Oct 1836 in Georgia. She died on 09 Jul 1904 in

Texas.

4.   iv. WILLIAM ARCHIBALD EDWARDS was born on 28 Feb 1835 in Talbot County, Georgia. He died on 12 Dec 1926 in Dallas, Texas. He married Eliza Jones White, daughter of Theophilus White and Mary H. Jett on 05 Jan 1858 in Russell County, Alabama. She was born on 08 Apr 1836 in Meriwether County, Georgia. She died on 06 Sep 1922 in Dallas, Texas.

5.   v. MARY CLEMENTINE EDWARDS was born on 06 Dec 1836 in Talbot County, Georgia. She died on 27 Sep 1871 in Statesville, Alabama. She married Mordecai White, son of Theophilus White and Mary H. Jett on 17 Mar 1853. He was born on 02 Sep 1829 in Brunswick County, Georgia. He died on 06 Jan 1896 in Autauga County, Alabama.

     vi. SARAH E. EDWARDS was born on 06 Aug 1838 in Talbot County, Georgia. She died in Jun 1849 in Alabama.

6.   vii. AMBROSE NEWTON EDWARDS was born on 21 Oct 1840 in Russell County, Alabama. He died on 20 Jul 1933 in Strawn, Texas. He married Joanna Columbia Ardis, daughter of Isaac Ardis and Jane Elizabeth White on 05 Dec 1865 in Dale County, Alabama. She was born on 04 Feb 1847 in Salem, Alabama. She died on 08 Aug 1922 in Greenville, Texas.

     viii. YOUNG MANSFIELD EDWARDS was born in May 1843 in Russell County, Alabama. He died on 22 Feb 1923 in Sulphur Springs, Hopkins County, Texas. He married Martha E. Ardis, daughter of Archibald McCoy Ardis and Joanna Leticia White on 05 Dec 1865 in Dale County, Alabama. She was born on 25 Feb 1843 in Russell County, Alabama. She died on 27 Jan 1903 in Brazoria County, Texas.

More About Young Mansfield Edwards:
Burial: 22 Feb 1923 in City Cemetery, Sulphur Springs, Texas, 1C, Lot 40
Cause Of Death: Kidney Failure (Brights Disease)
Occupation: 1870 in Bright Star, Texas (Present Day Sulphur Springs, Texas); School Teacher
Occupation: 1880 in Sulphur Springs, Texas; Merchant
Occupation: 1900 in Brazoria County, Texas; Farmer
Occupation: 1910 in Brazoria County, Texas; Farm Laborer
Occupation: 1920 in Sulphur Springs, Texas; None, living with his brother in law, Henry Love Ardis.
Military Service: Bet. 03 Jul 1861-09 Apr 1865 ; Company E. 15th Alabama Infantry, C.S.A.

Notes for Young Mansfield Edwards:
    Captured near Knoxville, Tennessee November 29, 1863 and imprisoned at Fort Delaware. Exchanged on October 10, 1864 and rejoined Company E, 15th Alabama Infantry, serving until the surrender of the Army of Northern Virginia at Appomattox Court House.

    Enlisted in Company E, 15th Alabama Infantry at Fort Mitchell, Alabama on July 3, 1861.

    Engagements: Winchester, Cross Keys, Cold Harbor, Malvern Hill, Cedar Mountain, Hazel River, Second Manasses Junction, Chantilly, Harper's Ferry, Sharpsburg, Fredricksburg, Suffolk, Battle Mount, Chicamauga, Raccoon

Mountain, Lookout Valley, Camel Station, Knoxville.

Wounded at Sharpsburg.and Fredricksburg.

Pre War residence was Westville, Alabama

Had no children.

ix.　JAMES CARTER EDWARDS was born on 20 Sep 1844 in Russell County, Alabama. He died about 1854.

7.　x. CHARLES ANDERSON BROWN EDWARDS was born on 25 Oct 1846 in Russell County, Alabama. He died on 23 Dec 1937 in Dothan, Alabama. He married Martha Caroline Crittenden, daughter of Cincinnatus Decatur Crittenden and Emeline Amanda Mahone on 01 Sep 1867 in Ozark, Alabama. She was born on 09 Feb 1851 in Schley County, Georgia. She died on 04 Apr 1929 in Ozark, Alabama.

8.　xi. WALTER STARR EDWARDS was born on 09 Sep 1850 in Russell County, Alabama. He died on 21 Sep 1927 in Geneva, Geneva County, Alabama. He married Sarah Frances Brown on 08 Jan 1871. She was born on 10 May 1853 in Georgia. She died on 30 May 1920 in Enterprise, Alabama.

Generation 2

2.　MARTHA LOUISE[2] EDWARDS (Ambrose[1]) was born on 20 Jul 1828 in Georgia. She died on 09 Aug 1881 in Alabama. She married Hope Hull Mizell, son of William Mizell and Mary Love on 07 Dec 1843 in Russell County, Alabama. He was born on 20 Sep 1820 in Baldwin County, Georgia. He died on 02 Mar 1887 in Haw Ridge, Alabama.

More About Martha Louise Edwards:
b: 20 Jul 1848
Burial: Haw Ridge, Alabama

More About Hope Hull
Mizell:
b: 20 Sep 1820
Burial: Ebenezer Cemetery, Dale County, Alabama
Occupation: 1850 in Russell County, Alabama; Farmer
Occupation: 1860; Farmer, Dale County, Alabama
Occupation: 1870; Merchant, Coffee County, Alabama
Occupation: 1880; Merchant, Haw Ridge, Alabama
Military Service: Dale County, Alabama, Home Guard, C.S.A.
Property: 1860 in Dale County, Alabama; 60 Acres Improved and 260 Acres Unimproved

Notes for Hope Hull Mizell:

Hope Hull Mizell and Martha Louise Edwards had the following children:

9.　i. WILLIAM CAPERS[3] MIZELL was born on 01 Oct 1844 in Russell County, Alabama. He died on 10 Sep 1934 in Ozark, Dale County, Alabama. He married Roxanna Chalker, daughter of William W. Chalker and Rebecca Anderson Land on 28 May 1871. She was born in 1848. She died on 27 Jan 1924 in Dothan, Houston County, Alabama.

ii.   EMELINE J. MIZELL was born about 1846 in Alabama. She married J.P. MARTIN.

10.   iii. ELVIRA ARIANNA MIZELL was born on 31 Mar 1851 in Coffee County, Alabama. She died on 01 May 1940 in Johnson County, Texas. She married Alfred Ward Kennon, son of Isham Kennon and Elizabeth (unknown) on 09 Apr 1868 in Haw Ridge, Alabama. He was born on 08 Jul 1847 in Alabama. He died on 20 Nov 1922 in Texas.

iv.   MARTHA L. MIZELL was born about 1855 in Alabama. She died on 20 Feb 1885 in Haw Ridge, Alabama. She married JOSEPH WILBURN STOKES. He was born on 29 Feb 1848 in Alabama. He died on 08 Jun 1922 in Dothan, Houston County, Alabama.

More About Martha L. Mizell:
Burial: 22 Feb 1885 in Haw Ridge Cemetery, Haw Ridge,

Alabama

Notes for Martha L. Mizell:

Reverend Angus Dowling conducted funeral service.

The Southern Star
Ozark, Dale County, Ala
. Wednesday, March 4, 1885

In Memoriam

In sadness we announce the death of Mrs. Fannie Stokes, wife of Mr. J.W. Stokes, of Haw Ridge, and daughter of Mr. H.H. Mizell. This mournful event transpired at her home, 3 p.m. Friday, 20th ult. Although she had been suffering for some months and her death seemed inevitable, yet when it came to pass many hearts were filled with sorrow and many eyes filled with tears. However, it affords relief from the bitterness of grief to know that she was so well prepared to meet the grim monster Death. She really died shouting victory over death and hell. Her last words were in praising and glorifying God her Savior. Her pure and sweet life gave assurance of triumph in death. She was pure in childhood, lovely in womanhood, a faithful Christian, a true member of the M.E. Church South, an affectionate daughter and sister, and a devoted wife and mother. She was buried in Haw Ridge graveyard Sunday morning, February 22, the Rev. Angus Dowling conducting the solemn and tearful service. A large assembly of weeping relatives and friends were present.

v.   FRANCES H. MIZELL was born about 1857 in Alabama.

vi.   AMBROSE E. MIZELL was born about Apr 1860 in Alabama.

vii.   HOPE HULL MIZELL was born on 04 Aug 1863 in Dale County, Alabama. He died on 09 Dec 1885 in Haw Ridge, Dale County, Alabama.

More About Hope Hull Mizell:
Burial: 10 Dec 1885 in Haw Ridge, Dale County, Alabama

Notes for Hope Hull Mizell:
   The Southern Star, Ozark, Dale County, Ala.
   Wednesday, December 16, 1885
   Page Two

   Hope Hull Mizell, son of H.H. Mizell and his sainted wife, was born near Pleasant Hill, Dale County, Ala., August 4th, 1863. During infancy he was dedicated to the Lord by baptism. Reared under the influence of a live church and trained by the example and instruction of truly pious parents, his character was formed and moulded into symmetrical beauty from childhood. Moral principles of purity and integrity were the foundations of his young and promising life.

   While yet a boy he realized the saving power of the grace of God, and joined the Methodist E. Church, South, at Haw Ridge, Ala. From that time forth he carefully and conscientiously observed and kept the rules and laws of the church. Besides, he intelligently obeyed the law of the spirit of life in Christ Jesus, which made him free from the law of sin and death. His life was a beautiful comment upon this glorious expression of the way of life everlasting. Thus, he was an epistle known and read of all men. He possessed the mind that was in Christ Jesus. He was a partaker of the divine nature. He was a child of God, an heir of God, and joint heir with Christ.

   As he grew in years he developed fine mental powers. His mind was fashioned and
beautified by careful, painstaking, mental culture. His mental powers were capable of almost indefinite expansion and force. He was well trained in exact thinking and reasoning.

   Such was the apparent case of his mental processes, that they seemed as intuitions. Thus endowed by nature and culture he was in public demand. He had reached ascending positions as a reliable business young man. When disease began to show its symptoms in the body of this promising young man, he was occupying a paying position in a good and growing house in the city of Troy, Alabama. Slowly, disease gained a deeper and stronger hold upon his manly form. Forced by physical disability he gave up his position, and came home to his father's house, in Haw Ridge, to suffer, linger and die. With patience divine, he endured to the end. No one ever heard a murmur of complaint escape his lips and yet no human power can express the depths and severe intensity of his suffering. Ready for the hour of departing, he looked beyond to the bright world of glory and loved ones. Among his last utterances, he bid his precious loved ones on earth to meet him in heaven. So he ascended to glory and home at 6 A.M. Wednesday, December 9th, 1885 aged 22 years, 4 months and 5 days. Thursday at 3 P.M. his body was laid to rest by the side of his glorified mother, at Haw Ridge. His burial was attended by a large company of loving and weeping relatives and friends. The service was conducted by the writer. Hope thou in God.

   Angus Dowling

   ----

viii.   LEROY M. MIZELL was born about 1868 in Alabama.

ix.   GEORGE PIERCE MIZELL was born on 23 Oct 1871 in Haw Ridge, Alabama. He died on 14 Mar 1954 in Waxahachie, Texas.

More About George Pierce Mizell:
Burial: 15 Mar 1954 in City Cemetery, Waxahachie, Texas

Cause Of Death: Congestive Heart Failure
Occupation: Insurance Representative

3. LEROY MARION[2] EDWARDS (Ambrose[1]) was born on 29 Aug 1830 in Talbot County, Georgia. He died on 24 May 1898 in Brundidge, Alabama. He married Martha Mizell, daughter of William Mizell and Mary Love on 06 Nov 1849 in Russell County, Alabama. She was born on 04 Feb 1829 in Houston County, Georgia. She died on 30 Oct 1908 in Brundidge, Pike County, Alabama.

More About LeRoy Marion Edwards:
Burial: Pleasant Hill Methodist Cemetery, Ozark, Alabama
Occupation: 1850 in Russell County, Alabama; Farmer
Occupation: Bet. 1860-1880 in Dale County, Alabama; Farmer,
Occupation: 1866; Justice of the Peace, Dale County, Alabama. Commissioned July 6, 1866.
Occupation: 1891; Justice of the Peace, Dale County, Alabama. Appointed January 29, 1891, Commisioned February 13, 1891.
Occupation: Bet. 1893-1895 Served in Alabama State Legislature
Occupation: 1894 in Dale County, Alabama; County Superintendant of Education. Elected August 6, 1894 and commisioned September 19, 1894.
Military Service: Bet. 26 Aug 1862-1865; Co. E, 53rd Alabama Mounted Infantry, C.S.A.
Property: 1850 in Russell County, Alabama; 20 Acres Improved and 60 Acres Unimproved
Property: 1860 in Dale County, Alabama; 60 Acres Improved and 100 Acres Unimproved
Property: 1870 in Dale County, Alabama; 160 Acres Improved and 140 Acres Unimproved

Notes for LeRoy Marion Edwards:
    Promoted to the rank of the rank of Second Lieutenant in Company E, 53rd Alabama Mounted Infantry on November 15, 1863. (Alabama Partisan Rangers).

    Enlisted August 26, 1862 and served until the end of the War.

    Served in Alabama State Legislature 1893-1895 Served
    as Justice of the Peace in Pike County, Alabama

    Died in the home of his daughter, Mary Love Edwards, while visiting her.

More About Martha Mizell:
Burial: Pleasant Hill Methodist Cemetery, Ozark, Alabama
Living In: 1900 Shellman, Randolph County, Georgia with her daughter Emeline and her family.

Notes for Martha Mizell:
Headstone gives March 4, 1828 for birth date. 1900 U.S. census gives February 1829 for birth. Headstone has October 30, 1908 for date of death.

More About LeRoy Marion Edwards and Martha Mizell:
Marriage License: 05 Nov 1849 in Russell County, Alabama
Marriage Fact: 06 Nov 1849 in Married by J. Scaife, Minister of the Gospel

LeRoy Marion Edwards and Martha Mizell had the following children:
        i. SARAH ELIZABETH[3] EDWARDS was born on 30 Oct 1849 in Russell County, Alabama. She died on 30 Mar 1863.

More About Sarah Elizabeth Edwards:
Burial: Pleasant Hill Methodist Cemetery, Ozark, Alabama

Notes for Sarah Elizabeth Edwards:
Sarah is listed on the 1850 U.S. census enumerated on January 25, 1850 as
one year old.
Headstone gives date of birth as October 30, 1851.

11. ii. MARY LOVE EDWARDS was born on 30 Dec 1851 in Russell County, Alabama. She died
on 05 Jul 1934 in Brundidge, Alabama. She married William Leroy Fleming, son of
John Alexander Fleming and Nancy Watson on 17 Jul 1873 in Dale County,
Alabama. He was born on 19 Apr 1848 in Harris County, Georgia. He died on 20 Feb
1920 in Pike County, Alabama.

iii. WILLIAM M. EDWARDS was born on 01 Apr 1853 in Dale County, Alabama. He
died on 28 Jul 1870 in Dale County, Alabama.

More About William M. Edwards:
Burial: Pleasant Hill Methodist Cemetery, Ozark, Alabama

12. iv. ARCHIBALD GAULDING EDWARDS was born on 01 May 1854 in Dale County, Alabama.
He died on 08 Oct 1903 in Enterprise, Alabama. He married Virginia Leonard
Crittenden, daughter of Cincinnatus Decatur Crittenden and Emeline Amanda
Mahone about 1876. She was born on 03 Oct 1857 in Georgia. She died on 11 Oct
1902 in Enterprise, Alabama.

13. v. EMELINE AMBROSE EDWARDS was born on 25 Jul 1855 in Dale County, Alabama. She
died on 02 Jan 1933 in Shellman, Georgia. She married Joashley Fernando
Crittenden, son of Cincinnatus Decatur Crittenden and Emeline Amanda Mahone
about 1877. He was born on 03 Mar 1855 in Georgia. He died on 14 Jun 1929.

vi. HENRY BASCON EDWARDS was born on 15 Mar 1857 in Dale County, Alabama. He
died on 23 Aug 1857 in Dale County, Alabama.

More About Henry Bascon Edwards:
Burial: Pleasant Hill Methodist Cemetery, Ozark, Alabama

vii. WARREN JAMES EDWARDS was born on 16 Feb 1858 in Dale County, Alabama. He
died on 19 Oct 1861 in Dale County, Alabama.

More About Warren James Edwards:
Burial: Pleasant Hill Methodist Cemetery, Ozark, Alabama

14. viii. AMBROSE JOHN EDWARDS was born in Apr 1859 in Dale County, Alabama. He died on
25 Jan 1938 in Enterprise, Alabama. He married MOENA BAMMA MATTHEWS. She was
born on 16 Nov 1858 in Dale County, Alabama. She died on 19 Mar 1915 in
Enterprise, Alabama. He married SARAH ANN CLARK. She was born on 19 Apr 1875 in
Alabama. She died on 29 May 1961 in Dothan, Alabama.

15. ix. LEROY MANSFIELD EDWARDS was born on 21 Oct 1870 in Dale County, Alabama. He died
in 1957. He married Charlotte Jane Morgan, daughter of George Morgan and

Rebecca Hall on 04 Feb 1893 in Dale County, Alabama. She was born in Apr 1870 in Alabama. She died on 05 Feb 1945 in Brewton, Escambia County, Alabama.

      x.   LORY J. EDWARDS was born about 1871 in Dale County, Alabama.

4.   WILLIAM ARCHIBALD[2] EDWARDS (Ambrose[1]) was born on 28 Feb 1835 in Talbot County, Georgia. He died on 12 Dec 1926 in Dallas, Texas. He married Eliza Jones White, daughter of Theophilus White and Mary H. Jett on 05 Jan 1858 in Russell County, Alabama. She was born on 08 Apr 1836 in Meriwether County, Georgia. She died on 06 Sep 1922 in Dallas, Texas.

More About William Archibald Edwards:
Burial: 14 Dec 1926 in Oak Cliff Cemetery, Dallas, Texas
Occupation: 1861; Farmer
Occupation: 1870 in Autauga County, Alabama; Minister
Occupation: 1880 in Farmersville, Texas; School Teacher
Occupation: 1900 in Eagle Ford, Dallas County, Texas; Minister
Occupation: 1910 in Dallas, Dallas County, Texas; Retired
Occupation: 1920 in Dallas, Dallas County, Texas; Retired - Living with his daughter Eliza and her husband George Cochran
Occupation: Methodist Minister
Military Service: Bet. 03 Jul 1861-13 Aug 1863; Company E, 15th Alabama Infantry, C.S.A.

Notes for William Archibald Edwards:

Published in:
Southern Star, Jan. 5, 1916

Dallas, Tex., Nov. 11, 1915. Dear Ruf:
    I wrote you for a list of my dear old Co. E. 15th Alabama Regiment who are now living, and as you were sick Bro. Charley Edwards sent me the following list vis.-W.R. Painter, W.C. Mizell Ozark; J.R. Edwards, Mat Williams, Ariton; C. V. Atkinson, Newton; Newt Curenton, Haw Ridge; Albert Austin, Daleville; W.D. Byrd, B.W. Fleming, Enterprise; Dorse Fleming, Geneva; C.G. Dillard, Ozark Route 1. To this I add the Texas list---Capt. Wm. A. Edwards, 4019 Bowser St. Dallas Texas; A.N. Edwards, Gordon, Tex.;Y.M. Edwards, Alvin, Tex.; J.P. Martin, Italy, Tex.; Ben Martin, Waxahachie, Tex.; Wm. Mobly Crandal Dallas County, Tex. The above constitute the list of survivors as I have it. If you know of any others please add them to this.
    The Company left home with 84 men enlisted all told 200. Returned home after surrender 100. So you see 100 brave and as good men as Dale or any other county ever raised sleep in some Northern or Southern cemetery or in shallow crude graves on some battle field, or possibly some were buried under the winter snow or to decay on some bloody hard fought battle ground and their bones to bleach under a burning sun, and to their dust and memory we say farewell dear comrades, and we hope some day to meet you beyond the flash and roar of artillery and rattle of musketry.
    It will probably be some interest to the friends and survivors of Co. E. to read a short write up of the Company which I hope you will have the Star to publish and send a copy to all living members. I t will likely be the last message they will ever get from me as I am now past eighty and they are not in their teens. I want each to take this as a personal letter and I would be glad to have a letter from all of them.
    No better Co. of citizen soldiers ever left any community than left Westville on the 18th day of July 1861, 54 years ago the past July. No more sumptuous feast was ever spread for departing patriots than was spread under the shade of the beautiful oaks that stood around old Darian Church. The loving hands that prepared it have long since been wafted beyond the curse of war and rage of battles by the angels of God. In all my life I have never seen deeper and purer emotions or heard

so tender farewells as followed that sumptuous feast. Husbands and wives embraced in tender love and with many it was the last embrace---fathers kissed their only babes---mothers threw a mothers arm around her son and with a mothers deep prayer sent her soldier boy to the conflict of battle and perils of war. And some of the boys felt the tender touch of the bride-to-be as they clasped hands that day. It thrilled their souls and nerved their arm for deeds of daring until they either perished in the campaign or returned home under the furled banner of the stars and bars. I have often been anxious to know if any of them that got back got left. "That day many parted, Where few shall meet."

That night we camped at Fraziers mill on Pea river and almost the entire company took a bath, and if there were either snakes, alligators or varmints for miles around they took to the hills and swamps never to return. Such a babel of voices and splashing of water I have never heard. The next night we camped in the open streets of Perote, and its bests families welcomed us with royal favors, and our third night out we stopped at Union Springs and spent the Sabbath there, which stay will always be kindly remembered by Co.E. That was the day of the first Manassas battle and Bull Run episode. Many thought the war was ended and some kind hearted mothers hoped their boys might see Richmond before they were disbanded. Well the boys saw Richmond and beyond. How little we knew of war and the bitter cup before the south.

We next find ourselves organized as Co. E. in the 15th Alabama Regiment. Nothing of special interest to the Co. E until our regiment camped at Camp Toombs between Centerville and Manassas. There Dick Neil died. This is worthy of mentioning because he was the first member of Co. E that died and the first one that had died in a regimental camp. He was honored as but few soldiers are ever honored. The Regiment was drawn up to witness the solemn burial, and Co. E with reversed arms and muffled drum followed the corpse to the road that leads from Centerville to Manassas; and there in plain coffin with a soldiers blanket for a winding sheet we buried him and a platoon of Co. E fired a soldier salute about the lonely grave, and there on the lonely spot unmarked by human hands and unknown to the busy world that passes that way to-day sleeps the dust of Corporal Neil without a stain on his name or character at home or in the army. It was the first crude shock that came to Co. E and it threw a gloom over the folks at home as nothing had done. All began to realize that war was on, and I remember at that camp Col. Canty told me it would be a terrible struggle. We spent the winter at Manassas and the only thing of special interest to Co. E was the task of getting boards for winter quarters, a task I never heard a single member complain of.

I was sent with my Company across Bull Run to the east of Centerville in the hilly and wooded country that had been but little occupied by soldiers up to that time, to get boards to cover huts for winter quarters. And old federal sympathizer lived about half a mile from our camp and killed hogs one day, it would have been better had he killed all he had. I went up to his house and wanted to buy a hasslet. He asked 50 cents for it and at that time we thought ten or fifteen cents good pay. I went back where the boys were at work and related what had occurred and I saw one of them give a significant wink and asked "Do you love hasslet Captain and I told him yes." Well to make a long story short, next morning when I woke up there was a ham of a 250 pound hog slipped under my tent and a large hasslet hanging in front and John Trawick, my cook, singing, whistling and frying liver and ham just as happy as he could get and you remember John could get very happy. I ate it and asked no questions for conscience sake, and as well as I remember it was the first and last stolen meat I ate during the war.

1862 was the fighting year of the war. Before the ground had thawed and the buds had burst into leaves we were taken from our pleasant quarters and transferred to the valley and received a formal introduction to Stonewall Jackson. There are two incidents in this campaign I wish to relate, not battles the historian does that, but unnoticed and unknown to the historian yet of interest to the Co. E. I allude to the death of Jno. Trawick and Lieut. Mills. John Trawick was killed almost under the guns of Harper Ferry, when we halted in our pursuit of Banks. We were resting on the turn-pike when a gun accidentally discharged and shattered poor Johns heel to pieces. He was carried to a Winchester Hospital, and in a few days I received notice he was dead.

I want to say this for John Trawick, I detailed him to cook for me, and he did more for my comfort than any one else has ever done. He carried my luggage on marches. (He was big and strong.) When the Regiment halted, if it was mid-night, he spread my bedding and cooked my supper no matter how tired he was, and I have often wondered if Israel's chariot was sent down to take that rough, rugged yet noble son of nature to a bright and better world.

Lieut. Mills was killed at Cross Keys, when an unexpected retreat was ordered our regiment. He was a hightoned, brave Christian gentlemen confided in at home and honored and loved in the army. He was devoted to his mess and his mess to him quiet, intelligent, refined and dignified a high type of a Christian gentleman yet he always impressed me that a cloud was over his spirits an I have never thought he expected to survive the war, and I thought and still think that terrible specter of presentment was ever before his eyes.

At night after the terrible battle of Gains Mills at Richmond after night fall had covered the field of carnage and death which was strewed with dead and dying, I fell on Billy Robinson, a fine specimen of manhood, tall, angular swarthy, hair as black as a crow and fearless as a lion. He told me he was mortally wounded and could live but a little while. He asked me who held the field I told him we held it. Then he said I am willing to die. Tell father I died fighting for my home and country, that I died brave and I feel I am prepared for a better world. His father was a Methodist preacher.

Co. E did the fighting for Hood's division at Suffolk. It held the line against great odds early morning till night, did the picket duty till mid night and covered the retreat of the army twenty or twenty five to Black Water River. I doubt if any Company ever withstood so strong and persistent attack, more courageously and firmly than did Co. E. A whole brigade against one company for an entire day, but we had the position on them.

During the engagement I met Jess Flowers, hat off sleeves rolled up, and sweat rolling from his brow. He said Captain they have killed my mess mate Cameron, and I am ready to fight the whole Yankee army. I believe Jess would have tried it. Cameron was a good man and soldier and died with his face to the enemy. The only three men I detailed to cook for me were Trawick, Flowers and Charley Jones; the two first were killed and Charley Jones crippled for life.

While we were at Suffolk, the battle of the wilderness was fought and fighting Joe Hooker whipped. Thence we followed Lee to Gettysburg, which with the surrender of Fort Donaldson sealed the fate of the Confederacy. They first brought Grant, the man of destiny into the lime light, and second, settled the question of invasion, and so reduced Lee's army that it was only a question of time when it would succumb to superior force. But I wish to say a few things about that great and fatal battle. First the 15th,
Alabama went further in that battle than any other troop, second Co. E went
as far as any part of the Regiment and staid as long. The men fired their guns until the
barrel become so hot they could not hold and load them.

The death of private Holloway was to me the saddest feature of this sanguinary struggle. We were well protected behind a great rock about 4 feet high, the enemy equally protected behind a rock fence not more than 50 yards in front of us, and Captain Park reported a flanking division (Sickles) coming in our rear. Col. Oats ordered a charge and mounted the rock himself and discharged the contents of a six shooter in the face of the enemy. No one would follow but Holloway who mounted the roch [rock], fell on his left knee, fixed his musket and a ball from the enemy crashed through his left temple and he fell dead on the feet of his gallant Colonel. How gallant! How useless! I saw the gallant deed and in the rage of battle and reign of death I thought what a sorrow it would carry to the bereaved wife and ten orphaned children far away in our beloved Alabama.

But our hearts were not always heavy and our heads bowed with grief. The soldier out of battle was ready for favor and the evening before the Gettysburg battle Co. E. was out on picket line.

Gen. Lee had ordered no private property disturbed and among the grove of large oaks in which [we] were camped a bunch of fine hogs had been browsing for acorns all day. Co. E's mouth had been watering all day for a taste of Yankee pork. Late that evening the Colonel told me there would be rations that evening and to let any one kill one of those hogs. I called the Co. together and told them to kill one of the biggest hogs and before I could stop then they had killed three and had a fourth so nearly dead I allowed them to finish it. But a very amazing thing occurred during the hog killing. I had two men in my Company, some of you may still remember them for no Company could well be without two such men. One was Sam Hog a great big over grown man, and Peters a small little fellow, and I looked out and saw Peters coming towards me closely pursued by Hog, nearly in touching distance and at every leap he would cry "help me Captain! Help me Captain." I called a halt-inquired the trouble, Hog said Peters hit him with a rock and nearly broke his leg, and Peters gasping for breath said "Captain you told us to kill the biggest hog we could find and he was the biggest one I saw. It was so ludicrous Hog burst into loud laughter and limping turned to his quarters. The truth was Peters had missed his mark.

One more incident that was very amusing to me, and the strange part isit never cease to be amusing to me. The parties to this incident were uncle Dave Snell and Latimer, both as true and worth men as ever girded their shoes with the accentments of war or shouldered a musket, both are now under
the soil beyond the din of battle.

One morning at roll call Latimer came up with a broken arm and it was broken after the rest of the Company had gone to bed, Uncle Dave was to report the case and with the usual gravity of old men. He said he and Latimer went to the spring to get water to cook and coming up from the spring with a bucket of water his foot slipped, he fell and broke his arm. No one dared question Uncle Dave's word, but it seemed strange to me they should be out at midnight after water to cook, I said nothing knowing full well if it had any rich or racy features the boys could not keep it from me. So I pretty soon got a full statement of the case, and not very much like Uncle Daves. They had gone to a nearby apple orchard and Latimer climbed a tree and sized a hornets nest and in his hasty retreat a limb broke, he fell and broke his arm. A few days after on the march I asked the old soldier to tell me exactly how the accident occurred and with great precision he related the affair to where Latimer started up the hill with his camp kettle of water and said "Captain he got slickest fall I ever saw." Well says I, Uncle Dave were there any hornets about the spring. "Captain he said I'll tell you all about it. I told him no I knew it all. I never blamed him not Latimer only for not knowing the difference between an apple and a hornet nest. In fact I never blamed Adam so much for eating that red apple Eve gave him, I expect I would have done as he did. This occurred as well as I remember at Raccoon ford of the Rapidam.

In conclusion of this article to my old true and tried friends and comrades-friends and soldiers tried in the concible [crucible?] of fire. There are a few things I reflect on with great pleasure.

1st, after the surrender Co. E returned from the scenes of battle and war, with true manhood and moral character and honest purpose entered honorable business and have been successful and useful citizens.

2nd, that my original mess eight of us are still living and constitute nearly half of the now living members of the Company.

3rd, and last and by far the most pleasing reflection is that I treated my Company as gentlemen, They were gentlemen at home and I could see no reason why they should not be treated as gentlemen in the army and I do not remember having punished one of my men, I consciously believed discipline could be maintained without it, and I do not believe the Confederacy ever produced a better Company on the march a more orderly one in camps, nor a braver one in battle, and soon the last of us will hear the tattoo for final sleep and rest, and the revile. When the trumpet of God shall awake and the sleeping dust of earths millions, and may we answer the roll call on that side of the river that makes glad the city of God.

Wm. A. EDWARDS

First Lieutenant July 3, 1861; Captain March 6, 1862; Resigned September 2, 1863 and served as Chaplain for the duration of the War.

Enlisted on July 3, 1861 at Fort Mitchell, Alabama and served until resigning to become Chaplain on September 2, 1863.

Engagements: Winchester, Cross Keys, Cold Harbor, Fredricksburg, Suffolk, Hazel River, 2nd Manassas, Chantilly, Harpers Ferry, Sharpsburg, Shepardstown, Gettysburg, Battle Mount.

Pre War residence was Westville, Alabama.

June 3-August 1, 1863 -- The Gettysburg Campaign.
No. 444.--Report of Col. William C. Oates, Fifteenth Alabama Infantry.

AUGUST 8, 1863.

SIR: I have the honor to report, in obedience to orders from brigade headquarters, the participation of my regiment in the battle near Gettysburg on the 2d ultimo. My regiment occupied the center of the brigade when the line of battle was formed. During the advance, the two regiments on my right were moved by the left flank across my rear, which threw me on the extreme right of the whole line. I encountered the enemy's sharpshooters posted behind a stone fence, and sustained some loss thereby. It was here that Lieut. Col. Isaac B. Feagin, a most excellent and gallant officer, received a severe wound in the right knee, which caused him to lose his leg. Privates (A.) Kennedy, of Company B, and (William) Trimner, of Company G, were killed at this point, and Private (G. E.) Spencer, Company D, severely wounded.

After crossing the fence, I received an order from Brigadier-General Law to left-wheel my regiment and move in the direction of the heights upon my left, which order I failed to obey, for the reason that when I received it I was rapidly advancing up the mountain, and in my front I discovered a heavy force of the enemy. Besides this, there was great difficulty in accomplishing the maneuver at that moment, as the regiment on my left (Forty-seventh Alabama) was crowding me on the left, and running into my regiment, which had already created considerable confusion. In the event that I had obeyed the order, I should have come in contact with the regiment on my left, and also have exposed my right flank to an enfilading fire from the enemy. I therefore continued to press forward, my right passing over the top of the mountain, on the right of the line.   On reaching the foot of the mountain below, I found the enemy in heavy force, posted in rear of large rocks upon a slight elevation beyond a depression of some 300 yards in width between the base of the mountain and the open plain beyond. I engaged them, my right meeting the left of their line exactly. Here I lost several gallant officers and men.

After firing two or three rounds, I discovered that the enemy were giving way in my front. I ordered a charge, and the enemy in my front fled, but that portion of his line confronting the two companies on my left held their ground, and continued a most galling fire upon my left.

Just at this moment, I discovered the regiment on my left (Forty-seventh Alabama) retiring. I halted my regiment as its left reached a very large rock, and ordered a left-wheel of the regiment, which was executed in good order under fire, thus taking advantage of a ledge of rocks running off in a line perpendicular to the one I had just abandoned, and affording very good protection to my men. This position enabled me to keep up a constant flank and cross fire upon the enemy, which in less than five minutes caused him to change front. Receiving reinforcements, he charged me five times, and was as often repulsed with heavy loss. Finally, I discovered that the enemy had flanked me on the right, and two regiments were moving rapidly upon my rear and not 200 yards distant, when, to save my regiment from capture or destruction, I ordered a retreat. Having become exhausted from fatigue and the excessive heat of the day, I turned the command of the regiment over to Capt. B. A. Hill, and instructed him to take the men off the field, and reform the regiment and report to the brigade.

My loss was, as near as can now be ascertained, as follows, to wit: 17 killed upon the field, 54 wounded and brought off the field, and 90 missing, most of whom are either killed or wounded. Among the killed and wounded are 8 officers, most of whom were very gallant and efficient men.

Recapitulation.--Killed, 17; wounded, 54; missing, 90; total, 161.

I am, lieutenant, most respectfully, your obedient servant,

W. C. OATES,
Colonel, Commanding Fifteenth Alabama Regiment

Lieut. B.O. PETERSON,
Acting Assistant Adjutant-General

See "NOTES" for Eliza Jones White for William Archibald Edwards autobiography.

More About Eliza Jones White:
d: 06 Sep 1922 in Dallas, Texas
Burial: 08 Sep 1922 in Oak Cliff Cemetery, Dallas, Texas

Notes for Eliza Jones White:
Oak Cliff Cemetery records give first name as "Elvira".

Autobiography
Or some incidents in my life
by Reverend William A.
Edwards (husband of Eliza Jones White)
Pate, Texas, 1897

I was born in Talbot County, Georgia on the 28th day of February, 1835. The day is designated in history as the cold Friday. It was the coldest day in the history of that country up to that date and I am sure that it has never been equaled since. It was said that the freeze was so powerful and deep that great trees of the forest burst and many of them died.

My father's name was Ambrose Edwards. He lived to be eighty-two years of age. My grandfather's name was William Edwards. He died at the age of eighty-four. I think he was born in the eastern part of Virginia and my impression is that he was the son of Ambrose Edwards.

My grandmother Edwards was Mary Whatley. I know very little of her family. I never saw any near kin on my grandmother's side of the house.

My father had a house built on his farm to take care of his parents in their old age. They had not occupied it more than a month before my grandmother died and grandfather then lived with his children, making his home with his youngest son, William Edwards.

My grandfather made a profession of religion and received the sacrament on his deathbed. My father, Ambrose Edwards, joined the Methodist Church at the age of twenty-five years and was one of the best men I ever knew.

My mother was Emeline James Gaulding, the daughter of John Gaulding. She died at the age of seventy-six. My grandfather Gaulding died of yellow fever in Mobile, Alabama when about sixty years old.

I never knew my grandmother Gaulding's maiden name or Christian name. I remember very distinctly seeing my father returning from the post office handing my mother a letter notifying her of the death of her father and the deep grief it produced on her refined and emotional nature. Mother died in the seventy-seventh year and both were buried in Westville, Dale County, Alabama.

My Edwards ancestors were robust in mind and body; were not afraid of anything; they nearly all acquired good property, but none of my father's family took much to books. On the other hand, my mother was a cultivated woman, about as much so as any raised in her day. The Gaulding family was cultivated and intelligent. Archibald Gaulding, the uncle for whom "A" in my name stands, was one of Georgia's most intelligent citizens. He was the most fascinating gentleman I nearly ever knew, as neat as a pin, as handsome as Absalom, as polite as Chesterfield, thoroughly educated, he was a man of mark. He served his state in the legislature, was a candidate for governor, but defeated, was for two terms auditor of the state road, and for many years, the State Masonic Lecturer and considered the brightest mason in the state.

I received my strong bodily constitution from the Edwards side and whatever taste or acquirements I may have in literature comes from my mother's family. I believe that my general knowledge exceeds that of any of my Edwards kin with whom I have met.

At the age of 14 I professed religion at Shady Grove Church in Lee County, Alabama. With my conversion came a clear call to the ministry, neither of which I have ever since doubted.

On the morning of the 5th day of January, 1858 I married Eliza Jones Mizell, the widow of James S. Mizell, and daughter of Theophilus White. We have raised eight children to be grown, two boys and six girls, all of them married. We have 27 grandchildren, six of which died, and as we grow older our life becomes more unified and happy. The names of our children are, respectfully: Theophilus Ambrose Edwards

Mary James Cora (Mrs. J. A. Skillern)

Annie Lee (Mrs. S. N. Neathery) Willie

Maud (Mrs. T. B. Lester) Mattie

Elizabeth (Mrs. B. L. Jones) Carrie

Louise (Mrs. J. L. Wilson)

Eliza (Lida) Emeline (Mrs. Geo. B.

Cochran) William Archibald Edwards, Jr.

There were no events in my childhood of unusual interest, I was considered forward, egotistical, and full of pranks and mischief, and a superabundance of life.

I cared little for books until my conversion and union with the church. From that day until the present books have been my best and most constant companion.

It seems to me now I must have been a boy of unusual endurance. I used to pick cotton all day and then hunt possums and coons with father's Negroes nearly all night. The first money I ever had was twenty-five cents and I paid it all for a money purse and then wore the purse out carrying it in my pocket and never had a cent to put in it. I next made fifty cents and bought a pistol with that and one day all left home but me and I spent the entire day shooting chickens and never hit one. I then swapped the pistol for an old vest and mother wouldn't let me wear it. That ended the speculation.

I felt the call to the ministry from the day of my conversion and I suppose I have made some of what the world would call sacrifices to preach. My uncle, for whom I was named, offered to give me a legal profession if I would accept it, but I felt I must preach. When I entered the ministry I was offered a law partnership with a guarantee of $2.500.00 for the first year with every prospect of a large increase and yet I declined it to enter the ministry and I am now at the age of sixty-two more than pleased with my choice. The lawyer that made the offer was in one of two years killed by a stroke of lightning and had I accepted the offer, some ill fatality might have befallen me ere this.

I supposed my war record will interest my family more than my ministry as the family is familiar with the latter.

Early in the summer of sixty I raised a company of volunteers, went to the war as its first lieutenant and was soon promoted to captain in which capacity I served until near the close of the war and received the appointment of missionary to the soldiers, resigned and came home. The immediate cause of my resignation was the promotion of Major Lowther to the Colonelcy, a man I had refused to serve under.

We left home for Virginia the 21st day of June. The day after the Battle of Bull Run was fought; we rendezvoused at the Ft. Mitchell near Columbus, Georgia and was organized in the 15th Alabama regiment as Company "E" and when we reached Virginia was placed in Trumble's Brigade, Ewell's Division, Army of Northern Virginia. Law afterward commanded the brigade and General J. B. Hood the division. We were under General Jackson in all of his valley campaigns and cooperated with Lee against McClellan in the seven days fight around Richmond. General Jackson's forces came from the Valley and struck to the rear of the Federal Army at Mechanicsville, six miles north of Richmond. In this battle General Ewell, I think, saved Lee's army from being routed by his presence and bravery. The confederates had almost fallen into a panic when the brave old man, with hat in hand, headed the retreating men crying at the top of his voice: "Men for God's sake, fight. You must fight, you must fight."

His presence and cheering words acted like magic. His men rallied a well nigh lost battle. I have never seen this stated in history, yet I always thought this saved the day. There were some incidents of this battle too pathetic not to mention. We slept that night on the battlefield, among the dead and dying. In wandering about in the dark to look for my men I stumbled on a dead man and by some strange impulse I stooped, passed my hand over his face and recognized him to be Andrew Wilson, a young man who had boarded at my father's and taught school. I called for a light, searched his person and found on him a fine gold watch, $2.00 in silver, which I sent home to his parents. I also found a cousin, his name was Carlisle, a noble youth and I always thought one of the most handsome men I ever saw. A minie ball had entered his left lung. He was sitting up with his head bowed forward and ever and anon, the gurgling sound told the sad tale that life was rapidly passing away. He was suffering intensely. I asked him if he knew me. He said "It's Cousin Billie". I asked him if I could help him and he muttered rather indistinctly "water". I took a canteen of water from a dead man and I held it to his mouth and he drank freely of it. I saw all was over with him, that I could do no more for him. I left him to struggle alone in the dark with none to soothe or comfort and I have always indulged the hope that an angel carried his noble and brave soul beyond the conflict of armies and the cruelty of war.

There was yet another touching incident in this night ramble among the dead. I had a private soldier, W. C. Robinson, in my Company. He was the son of an old itinerant Methodist preacher of the Alabama Conference. I called out "15 Alabama" and not far off he answered, "here". I asked "Is this you Billy?" He said, "Yes". I said, "Are you much hurt?" He replied, "I am killed." I found a minie ball had passed through the body and that his statement was too true. He said, "Who holds the battlefield". He faced danger with the chivalry of the bravest knight and death with the placidity of the bravest Christian.

I was on the second Maurn battleground ten days after the battle. No Federal soldiers had been buried. They were in a state of putrefaction and were distended almost to the condition of bursting. Thousands of these poor fellows lay on the ground, in some places I could have walked for hundreds of yards on the dead and Federal troops had turned as black as a Negro which they invariably did in a few hours after they were killed. It was a phenomena the Confederates did not turn black. This was not only a dreary, revolting spectacle, but seen just at night, was a frightful sight.

I saw an old excavation cut in a railroad, hundreds of Yankee soldiers killed together not covered with earth.

The confederates had been buried, but in a small clump of oak trees I found one confederate soldier. Evidently he had been dead but a few hours and, no doubt, he died from neglect and starvation. I paused, looked at the little pile of bones and emaciated manhood and in the sympathy of my soul said here lies a noble dead, perhaps brave and good and yet no marble slab will ever mark his resting place and no wife or mother will ever learn of his painful and lingering death.

The battleground was under a flag of truce and that night I slept in some house with at least a dozen volunteers and army surgeons.

We waded the Potomac River to get to the Battle of Gettysburg and returning crossed on pontoons. There are some facts in this battle I have not seen in history. The 15th Alabama Regiment was the extreme right of General Lee's. Just as we began the attack Hood was wounded and Law took command of the division. Our regiment crept over Big Round Top Mountain and fought until all our ammunition was exhausted and for want of reinforcement and ammunition was compelled to retire.

In this battle I saw General Bulger shot through the body. He fell like a dead man and after the war I met the same gentleman. He was a candidate for Governor of the State of Alabama.

I saw Colonel Oates, since Governor of Alabama, mount a rock within thirty yards of the enemy and discharge the contents of a repeater in their face.

When we began the retreat back across the mountains the Federals were pressing and I was exhausted and with my third lieutenant and private soldier, slipped into a cave in the side of the mountain and about midnight came out, located the pickets by the firing and crowded between their post which was about a hundred yards apart and reached our command in safety. I am satisfied I went as far toward Washington as any other Southern soldier.

On many of our campaigns we often waded rivers from waist to neck deep and that we might stem the current we walked, four abreast, and with arms around each other, constituted mutual support. I had a very narrow escape at Suffolk on the southern side of Richmond. I was in command of a long line of pickets and had the advantage of a dense line of timber that covered us from view of the enemy. The line was at least eight hundred yards long and my left wing gave way while I was at the right and I ran in between my own men and the enemy who had then entered the woods and had driven my forces back. I found myself within a hundred yards of a solid line of Federal Soldiers, but as the woods were dense I do not think they ever saw me. I found my command had secured a good position about five hundred yards back and quietly awaited my coming.

The army began its retreat at dark and I was left on duty with orders to withdraw at one A.M.

sharp and cover the retreat to Black Water, twenty-five miles, which I did without loss of a man and in perfect order. In that fight I lost several of my best men. One soldier whose name was Cameron was killed and my detailed cook, Jesse Flowers*, carried him back to a camp and his body now rests in an old field pine thicket near Suffolk, Virginia. Flowers met me on his return with his sleeves rolled up to his elbows and said, "Captain, they have killed my old mess mate and best friend and I am now ready to fight until they kill me or I kill some of them." Soon the news came to me that Jesse Flowers was killed. By the side of his friend they buried him. Two braver soldiers never shouldered a musket or wore the Confederate gray. I wish I could indulge in the hope that they might arise with the just. But Flowers was wicked and Cameron, I think, was not religious, so I throw the mantle of oblivion over these two men and await the revelation of the great hereafter.

The three best friends I had in the army or ever had, all met their death in the same way. One was Lieutenant Patten who took camp fever at Manassas in 1861 and was transferred to a hospital at Richmond and soon I received notice he was dead. He was a gentleman of intelligence and a friend that never faltered or flickered. When he left I felt like I should never see him again and too soon my forebodings were realized. He was a wicked man and the last word I ever heard from him before the final farewell was an oath. It is probable he may have had a death bed repentance and from his narrow and crude little bunk gone up to a wider and better berth.

The second was John Trawick. I detailed him as a cook. He was shot accidentally in the foot in the valley near Harper's Ferry and died in a hospital at Winchester. John Trawick was a poor man, illiterate, unmannerly, profane and dissipated and yet he would do more for me and my comfort than any man living or dead. After the hardest wars and battles he would never sleep, though we might not reach camp until 12 or 1 o'clock at night, until he had prepared my supper, no matter how I protested. I am ashamed to say after the lapse of thirty years how much Mr. Trawick did for me.

Florence was the third and as I have already spoken freely of him, I will let that suffice.

My work as missionary was to the troops of Florida. My headquarters were scattered from the mouth of the Sewanee River to St. Andrews Bay, from Marian to the nearest point on the coast was from fifty to sixty miles and there was but one human habitation between.

I took my wife and oldest child on one trip. We stayed all night at the midway house. It was a pole hut, twelve by fourteen; one room, besides my family there was another family of eleven persons and I have never yet found out how we all slept as the night was cold. One thing I remember, the man took quite a fancy to Mrs. Edwards and gave her a fine venison ham as we returned home.

There were many dense thickets or "Tight Eye Swamps" in all that country and served as an impregnable fortress for hostile deserters. I never passed one of these that I did not feel I was in great danger. I expected to hear the deserters' rifles from these thickets every time I passed them. I suffered far more uneasiness than I did in the regular army.

Returning from one of my tours to the post at St. Andrews Bay I met an army composed of Yankees, Negroes and deserters, they raided Marian, burned a part of the town and killed some of its citizens. It was ten miles out they leveled their guns on me. I thought as I had no weapon and was outnumbered I had better surrender. They carried me ten miles further towards the coast and then took my horse, the best one I ever owned, and turned me loose on foot with a pair of heavy saddle pockets and seventy miles from home and twenty from anywhere else. On foot I started home. Almost the entire way either exposed to danger from the deserters or negroes loafing around, whose owners had run out of the country and they were imprudently occupying it.

In going from my home in south Alabama to the troops in Florida I had a stopping place with a Mrs. Clark. One evening just before sundown I met her and her little girl about two miles from her house. She told me I had better turn back that 300 deserters were camped at her house and they would either kill or badly mistreat me if I went on. I asked her if she could take care of me, she said she would try. I turned, rode back to her sister's and they held a consultation and decided to send or carry me to Mrs. Reed's, a deserter's wife, who lived in the lone pine woods back from the public road. These ladies said if the deserters came to Mrs. Reed's she would claim me as her guest and save me. Mrs. Reed agreed to take me and do the best she could for me. She lived in a pole cabin with open cracks as large as your arm. She fed me that night on boiled sweet potatoes which was the best and all she had for my horse was peas. It was a bright moonlight night, here was a brilliant fire of lightwood on the hearth and I sat leaning back by a large crack in the chimney corner. I looked out and saw a line of deserters at least a hundred armed with shotguns and muskets coming right to my back. I asked the lady if it would not be safer if I moved. She said that would create suspicion and cause them to stop and if I did not move they would most likely pass on. I don't think I ever sat so still before or since or covered so little space. That night they attacked the county seat, Newton, fifteen miles away. Four were killed and so many wounded.

After the surrender there were marauders robbing and hanging men friendly to the war and supposed to have money and I had been told I would share a similar fate. So we gave our valuables to our cook, Hogue, among other things a $150.00 gold watch and I took a Negro boy, Lewis, a bed quilt and shotgun and went out in a thicket near the house determined if they came to have the advantage of being on the outside. After we had been up for about an hour I said, "Lewis, I will go to sleep and you watch and if anybody comes you wake me." "Yes, sah, Marse Billy, if any man hurts you this night he will have to first walk over my dead body."

I went to sleep and woke the next morning with Lewis sleeping by my side, enjoying a full share of the quilt with me. I never asked Mrs. Edwards how she spent the night, but I guess she was as good to the cook as I was to Lewis. This was the last uneasy night I ever spent on account of war.

The last transaction I ever had in Confederate money I sold a calf skin for $300.00.

I was, at one time, offered a position on the weather bureau with a salary of $1,500.00 and the rank of captain if I would be mustered into service. I declined it. There were times when I had flattering prospects as a preacher, but that is all gone now. I once had offers and temptations to other pursuits, but that is all gone.

An Arab once rode a fine horse in front of an English officer and the Englishman offered him such tempting prices for his animal he galloped away from it to get out of his reach.

So I have gone out of the way of temptations. I have not done it as the Arab, but Old Time has mounted me and has rode me beyond the flattering offers and temptations of the world and now I keep my eye on the mark for the prize of the high calling of God in Christ Jesus.

****

Thirty years have passed. I
am ninety years old today.
I have broken the family record.

My father died at 82 and my mother at 76, a pretty fair record for longevity. Besides my immediate family I have forty-five grandchildren.

One thing dominated me as far back as I can remember, a determination never to grow old, that is never to have old folk's ways, to be a boy in spirit through life and I do not think I have ever risen much above a boy in any respect. I suppose I have been what the world would call an optimist, that is, a man that hasn't anything and doesn't want anything. I think I had my duplicate in an old farmer in Alabama. He had forty acres of $3.00 per acre of land, and a possum dog and said he would not take forty thousand dollars for it. To me every picture of life has two sides and I have always turned the bright side to my gaze. I have always taken a forward look. The fate of Lot's wife early impressed me with the backward look.

I have preferred Paul's rule of action, forgetting the things that are behind.

Seventy-two years ago I joined the Methodist Church and my name was never off the church roll or the conference roll since.

I have been preaching sixty-four years and in all these years I have done many things I should not have done and left many things undone.

I think I can say today before the Good Father in whose presence I must soon appear I have always been loyal to Christ. I have confessed Him before me. I have taken the Christian side of every moral issue in life that has come before the public for action.

I joined the Alabama Conference and filled pastorates there as follows: Central Institute, Autaugaville, Ivey Creek, Summerfield and Day. I remained in that conference ten years, then transferred to the North Texas Conference, November 17, 1875. Served the Sulphur Springs Circuit; and Greenville Station. Located in December, 1876. For several years I taught school near Greenville, 1876 to 1880. Farmersville, 1880 to 1884. Lewisville, 1884 to 1886.

In 1886 I was readmitted into the North Texas Conference. My pastoral charges were Collinsville, Mt. Pleasant, Atlanta, Kaufman, Wills Point, Cochran and Caruth, Royse City, Fate, West Dallas, Haskell Avenue and Princeton. Fifty years of my ministry was spent in Texas and thirty-five years of this time was spent preaching in and around Dallas. I have seen the M. E. Church South grow from 455,000 members to two and one quarter million.

On March 1, 1925, I was made Chaplain General of the Trans-Mississippi Department of the

United Confederate Veterans which was a distinctive honor to me.

I am proud of my country, my church, and my family and the age in which I live.
****

My father passed away on December 12, 1926. He had reached the age of 91 years and 10 months.

He preached on his 90th birthday at the Oak Lawn Methodist Church on Cedar Springs and Oak Lawn Avenue.

On his 91st birthday, February 28, 1925, he preached at the Oak Cliff Methodist Church on Jefferson Street.

He was looking forward to preaching at the invitation of Dr. Gregory at First Methodist Church on the corner of Ross Avenue and Harwood on his 99th birthday.

He preached at Lakewood Methodist Church just one week before his death.

He was a frequent writer to the Texas Christian Advocate and to the Dallas Morning News. A friend has said of him:

"Brother Edwards had all the charm of a cultured Christian gentleman. He was a reader of good books. He thought out the fundamental questions. He wrote with ease and always illuminatingly. He prepared thoroughly his own discourses and he expected the preacher to whom he listened to give a message of strength and clearness. He lived here far beyond the limit of most men, but he lived to the last with full purpose. He was loved and cherished in his own home and by his brethren and friends. He passed on to his glorious crown with God's grace, resting upon him and with peace and good will abounding towards all men. We shall see him again."

Mrs. George A.
Cochran 2019 Bowser
Avenue Dallas, Texas

More About William Archibald Edwards and Eliza Jones White:
Marriage License: 04 Jan 1858 in Russell County, Alabama
Marriage Fact: Married by John C. Ardis, M.G.

William Archibald Edwards and Eliza Jones White had the following children:

16.   i. THEOPHILUS AMBROSE[3] EDWARDS was born on 17 Jul 1859 in Dale County, Alabama. He died on 11 Feb 1929 in Dallas, Texas. He married Nora Elizabeth Bumpass, daughter of William Presley Bumpass and Mariah Hungerford Thomas on 26 Dec 1882 in Collin County, Texas. She was born on 26 Sep 1858 in Sulphur Springs, Texas. She died on 19 Apr 1927 in Grand Prarie, Texas.

17.   ii. MARY JAMES CORA EDWARDS was born on 06 Sep 1864 in Dale County, Alabama. She died on 15 Jul 1935 in Bella Vista, Arkansas. She married James Arthur Skillern, son of William Franklin Skillern and Sarah Ann Henninger on 04 Nov 1884 in Lewisville, Texas. He was born on 29 May 1856 in Pikeville, Tennessee. He died on 29 Dec 1914 in Dallas, Texas.

18.   iii. ANNIE LEE EDWARDS was born on 08 Nov 1867 in Alabama. She died on 22 Apr 1908 in Haskell, Texas. She married Stephen Nathaniel Neathery, son of Allen Hill Neathery and Elizabeth Jemima Buie on 30 Dec 1884 in Denton County, Texas. He was born on 16 Jan 1864 in Texas. He died on 22 Nov 1943 in Haskell, Texas.

19.   iv. WILLIE MAUD EDWARDS was born on 22 Aug 1868 in Autauga County, Alabama. She died on 04 Aug 1946 in Dallas, Texas. She married Thomas Benton Lester on 03 Dec 1886 in Caddo, Indian Territory (Oklahoma). He was born on 29 Feb 1856 in Mississippi. He died on 13 Apr 1928 in Dallas, Texas.

20.   v. CARRIE LOUISE EDWARDS was born on 30 Sep 1871 in Autaugaville, Alabama. She

died on 25 Nov 1971 in Albuquerque, New Mexico. She married James Lee Wilson, son of William Henry Wilson and Elizabeth C. Pickens on 27 Feb 1889 in Mt. Pleasant, Texas. He was born on 09 Mar 1863 in Franklin, Holmes County, Mississippi. He died on 23 Jan 1917 in Celina, Collin County, Texas.

21.   vi. MATTIE ELIZABETH EDWARDS was born on 30 Sep 1871 in Autaugaville, Alabama. She died on 15 Oct 1969 in Dallas, Texas. She married Benjamin Lee Jones, son of William Edwards Jones and Lonette Holcombe on 27 Feb 1889 in Mt. Pleasant, Texas. He was born on 18 Mar 1862 in Collinsville, Texas. He died on 17 Sep 1937 in Dallas, Texas.

22.   vii. ELIZA EMELINE EDWARDS was born on 09 Sep 1874 in Summerfield, Alabama. She died on 20 Jan 1964 in Dallas, Texas. She married George Henry Cochran, son of James Monroe Cochran and Margaret Lively on 30 Oct 1895 in Dallas, Texas. He was born on 04 Oct 1870 in Dallas, Texas. He died on 05 Apr 1956 in Dallas, Texas.

      viii. WILLIAM ARCHIBALD EDWARDS was born on 24 May 1876 in Greenville, Texas. He died on 22 Aug 1915 in Dallas, Texas. He married India May Hughes on 12 Jul 1899 in Atlanta, Texas. She was born on 21 Sep 1875 in Tennessee. She died on 29 Oct 1963.

More About William Archibald Edwards:
Burial: 24 Aug 1915 in Oak Cliff Cemetery, Dallas,
Texas Cause Of Death: Tuberculosis
Living In: 1910 Living with Frank and Elizabeth Skillern in Dallas, Texas.
Occupation: 1900 in Atlanta, Cass County, Texas; Commercial Traveller (Travelling Salesman)
Occupation: 1910 in Dallas, Dallas County, Texas; Travelling Salesman, American Soda Company

5.   **MARY CLEMENTINE[2] EDWARDS** (Ambrose[1]) was born on 06 Dec 1836 in Talbot County, Georgia. She died on 27 Sep 1871 in Statesville, Alabama. She married Mordecai White, son of Theophilus White and Mary H. Jett on 17 Mar 1853. He was born on 02 Sep 1829 in Brunswick County, Georgia. He died on 06 Jan 1896 in Autauga County, Alabama.

More About Mary Clementine Edwards:
Burial: Love Family Cemetery, Mulberry, Autauga County, Alabama

Notes for Mary Clementine Edwards:
Died of burns received while protecting her children when a kerosene lamp exploded.

More About Mordecai White:
Burial: Love Family Cemetery, Mulberry, Autauga County, Alabama
Cause Of Death: pneumonia
Occupation: 1850 in Russell County, Alabama; Teaching
Occupation: 1860 in Dale County, Alabama; Clerk
Occupation: 1870 in Henry County, Alabama; Dry Goods Merchant
Occupation: 1892; Member of State Legislature from Autauga County, Alabama
Military Service: Bet. 02 Mar-23 Dec 1863; Company I, 57th Alabama Infantry, C.S.A.

Notes for Mordecai White:

Served as Captain of Company I, 57th Alabama Infantry from March 21, 1863 until he resigned for health reasons on December 23, 1863.

Headstone has his name as Mordica White.

Mordecai White and Mary Clementine Edwards had the following children:

    i. LILLY D.[3] WHITE was born on 19 Apr 1855 in Alabama. She died on 06 Aug 1875. She married ISAAC NEWTON NUNN.

        More About Lilly D. White:
        Burial: Love Family Cemetery, Mulberry, Autauga County, Alabama

    ii.   ROBERT H. WHITE was born on 23 Mar 1857 in Alabama. He died on 12 Aug 1874.

        More About Robert H. White:
        Burial: Love Family Cemetery, Mulberry, Autauga County, Alabama

    iii. EMELINE J. WHITE was born about 1859 in Alabama. She married (UNKNOWN) WHETSTONE.

    iv. THEOPHILUS WHITE was born on 19 Feb 1861 in Alabama. He died on 01 Aug 1874.

        More About Theophilus White:
        Burial: Love Family Cemetery, Autauga County, Alabama

23.   v. AMBROSE PATRICK WHITE was born on 15 Apr 1863 in Westville, Alabama. He died on 04 Jan 1933 in Ozark, Alabama. He married Henrietta Anderson Chalker, daughter of William W. Chalker and Rebecca Anderson Land on 06 Jan 1886 in Westville, Alabama. She was born on 11 Jan 1860 in Westville, Alabama. She died on 04 May 1943 in Ozark, Alabama.

24.   vi. THOMAS D. WHITE was born in Mar 1865 in Alabama. He married Emma Coleman in May 1890 in Greenwood, Florida. She was born in Feb 1864 in Ala bama.

    vii. WILLIAM WHITE was born about 1868 in Dale County, Alabama. He died in 1892 in Iowa Park, Texas.

    viii. YOUNG MANSFIELD WHITE was born on 28 Jan 1869 in Alabama. He died on 09 Jun 1952 in Prattville, Alabama. He married MARY JONES. She was born on 27 Aug 1873 in Alabama. She died on 02 Jul 1945 in Alabama.

        More About Young Mansfield White:
        Burial: Ivy Creek United Methodist Cemetery, Autaugaville, Autauga County, Alabama
        Occupation: 1900 in Mulberry, Autauga County, Alabama; Farmer
        Occupation: 1910 in Mulberry, Autauga County, Alabama; Farmer
        Occupation: 1920 in Mulberry, Autauga County, Alabama; Farmer
        Occupation: 1930 in Mulberry, Autauga County, Alabama; Farmer
        Occupation: 1940 in Mulberry, Autauga County, Alabama; Florida

ix.   MARY C. WHITE was born on 24 Jul 1871 in Alabama. She died on 10 Oct 1871.

More About Mary C. White:
Burial: Love Family Cemetery, Mulberry, Autauga County, Alabama

6.   **AMBROSE NEWTON**[2] **EDWARDS** (Ambrose[1]) was born on 21 Oct 1840 in Russell County, Alabama. He died on 20 Jul 1933 in Strawn, Texas. He married Joanna Columbia Ardis, daughter of Isaac Ardis and Jane Elizabeth White on 05 Dec 1865 in Dale County, Alabama. She was born on 04 Feb 1847 in Salem, Alabama. She died on 08 Aug 1922 in Greenville, Texas.

More About Ambrose Newton Edwards:
Burial: 21 Jul 1933 in Forest Park Cemetery, Greenville, Texas- Moved later to Restland Cemetery, Dallas, Texas
Cause Of Death: Prostate Cancer
Occupation: 1860 in Dale County, Alabama; School Teacher
Occupation: 1870 in Sulphur Springs, Texas; Dry Goods Merchant
Occupation: 1880 in Hopkins County, Texas; County Clerk
Occupation: Bet. 27 Mar 1886-20 Oct 1891 ; Postmaster, Eliasville,
Texas
Occupation: 1900 in Palo Pinto County, Texas; Lumber Dealer
Occupation: 1910 in Gordon, Palo Pinto County, Texas; Lumber
Merchant
Occupation: 1920 in Palo Pinto County, Texas; Retired
Occupation: 1930 in Greenville, Texas; Retired - Living with his son, Ambrose Edwin Edwards
Military Service: Bet. 03 Jul 1861-11 Jun 1865 in C.S.A.; Company E, 15th Alabama Infantry

Notes for Ambrose Newton Edwards:
    Enlisted on July 3, 1861 in Westville, Alabama and served until July 2, 1863 when he was captured at Gettysburg, Pennsylvania and made a prisoner of war. Sent first to Fort McHenry, Maryland on July 5, 1863 and then to Fort Delaware, Delaware on July 6, 1863. Released from Fort Delaware on June 11, 1865.

    Engagements: Winchester, Cross Keys, Harpers Ferry, Sharpsburg, Fredricksburg, Suffolk, Malvern Hill, Cedar Mt. Hazel River, 2nd Manassas, Chantilly, Gettysburg.

    Wounded at Sharpsburg.and Fredricksburg.

    Promoted to Second Sergeant May 15, 1862.
    Promoted to First Sergeant July 25, 1862.
    Promoted to Second Lieutenant but was captured at Gettysburg, Pennsylvania before his commission arrived.

    Pre Civil War Residence was Westville, Alabama.

    Flag of the Army of Northern Virginia covered his casket during his first funeral and burial at Greeneville, Texas.

    Member of the first Board of Regents for the University of Texas 1881-1882

    Buried in Greenville, Texas in 1933 and then buried in Restland Cemetery, Dallas, Texas on February 9, 1955, grave marker set on August 31, 1955.

    Became a Mason at Brightstar Lodge number 221 in Sulphur Springs, Texas on November 5, 1868.

Death certificate gives October 18, 1840 as date of birth.

Dictated to Emma Irene Garland (Edwards) in 1930

I well remember the day when my company assembled at old Darian Church in Dale County, Alabama, where we bade good bye to our loved ones and took up our march to the battle front in answer to our country's call.

I remember the first night we camped on the banks of Pea River and bathed in its waters and spent this our first night in joyous hilarity. I remember after three days march we reached old Fort Mitchell near Columbus Georgia, where we were organized into the 15th Alabama Infantry, my company being known as co. E. Then after a few weeks of company and regimental drill we had orders to go to Virginia, and this was for me a matter of exquisite thrill and interest which cannot be well depicted here.

When we reached Richmond we were quartered at Old Chimborozo where we remained about three weeks and thence to Manassas. Shortly after the noted first battle of the war, as there was no more fighting in this section, we went into winter quarters there. Up to this time we had not had to suffer any great hardships, but had many interesting experiences.

In the beginning of 1862, the second year of the war, greater activities in war matters became more tense. McClelland was assembling a great army in the Yorktown peninsula with the purpose of marching on to Richmond and General Johnson was ordered to fall back from Manassas to meet this move of the enemy. But Ewell's division, to which I belonged, was ordered to join Stonewall Jackson in the valley. Then my regiment was in the noted Valley campaign in which Jackson defeated three armies and then it was at Cross Keys we received our baptism of battle. From here the scene changed and the Seven days battle around Richmond was fought in which my regiment took an active part and lost quite a number of noble men.

I was sick and in the hospital at Charlottesville at that time. After McClelland's defeat General Lee moved his army North. On the first invasion. we crossed the Potomac at Leesburg, wading it of course as there were no bridges. My division was ordered to go around and cross back above Harper's Ferry where General Wool was stationed with seven thousand men. We had him completely surrounded and he surrendered. In this surrender we secured arms, commissary, and quarter master supplies in great abundance.

Immediately after the surrender we were ordered back across the Potomac to be in the battle of Sharpsburg - called Antetim by the North Historians - this was one of the hardest battles of the war, and was known as a draw. Lee withdrew to the Virginia side and there ended that year's campaign in Virginia.

To avoid being tedious, I will omit many important military operations including the battle of Fredericksburg in which i took a part and will speak of the Pennsylvania invasion and the battle of Gettysburg. I was in this battle and on the second day of July 1863, with thirteen other men of my company was captured and carried to Fort Delaware where we were kept as prisoners until the war closed.

I could make an interesting chapter about our prison, but only say we managed to keep up spirit and hope amid its trials and troubles until the day came for our release nearly two months after the surrender.

I reached home on the 5th of June 1865, to find our beloved Southland wrecked and ruined by war's devastation.

Then it was with unflinching courage we took up the task of reconstructing the ruin and building our new South upon it. While I cannot elaborate on this work, for it would require many words, yet I cannot omit saying that the work was done in a way that solicited the admiration of all people. Our noble women were our staunch co-laborers in every sence, and deserve a monument for their wonderful work.

On the 5th of December 1865 it was my good fortune to lead to the marriage alter one of the best of the noble daughters of the South, to walk with me and share with me, every joy and every sorrow that awaited us on life's pilgrimage. We came to Texas in 1866 where eight sons came to bless our union, all noble men and all living useful lives in Texas except one. Eight years ago my precious one left me to go and wear her crown.

Now in my 90th year I can truly say that much love and kindness have been meted out to me, but must say that the best friends we old veterans have are the noble Daughters of the Confederacy, and may god bless them in my closing word.

A. N. Edwards
Co. E. 15th Alabama Inf.

More About Joanna Columbia Ardis:
Burial: 08 Aug 1922 in Forest Park Cemetery, Greenville, Texas- Moved later to Restland Cemetery, Dallas, Texas
Cause Of Death: Stomach Cancer

Notes for Joanna Columbia Ardis:
Re buried in Restland Cemetery, Dallas, Texas on February 9, 1955, grave marker set on August 31, 1955.

Ambrose Newton Edwards and Joanna Columbia Ardis had the following children:

25.   i.   ISAAC MANSFIELD[3] EDWARDS was born on 01 Feb 1868 in Strawn, Texas. He died on 18 Mar 1945 in Strawn Texas. He married Mary Sophronia (Onie) Strawn, daughter of Stephen Bethel Strawn and Emeline Jane Allen in 1899 in Palo Pinto County, Texas. She was born on 11 Apr 1874 in Strawn, Texas. She died on 18 Feb 1950 in Temple, Bell County, Texas.

     ii.   WALTER WHITE EDWARDS was born on 31 Oct 1870 in Sulphur Springs, Texas. He died on 27 Nov 1938 in El Paso, Texas. He married Mary Anna King, daughter of Porter King and Eudorah Martha Bush in 1897 in Palo Pinto County, Texas. She was born on 23 Jul 1864 in Texas. She died on 23 Dec 1956 in Amarillo, Potter County, Texas.

More About Walter White Edwards:
Burial: 29 Nov 1938 in Evergreen Cemetery, El Paso, Texas
Cause Of Death: Cardiac Failure, Hypertension
Occupation: 1910; Gold Miner, Gorden, Palo Pinto County, Texas
Occupation: 1920; Salesman, El Paso, Texas
Occupation: 1930; Geologist, El Paso, Texas

Notes for Walter White
Edwards:
Dear Mr. Edwards:
Your request to our Geological Information Center for information on the Baking Powder mine was forwarded to me. Probably fewer than a half-dozen living people in all the southwest have even heard of
this property as it is one of the more obscure such in all New Mexico. I am not aware that the property was ever examined by a trained geologist or engineer (unless your Edwards relatives were such and there is no known surviving record of their work). My extensive mines and prospects files are absolutely silent in regard to the Baking Powder. Nevertheless I have noted one or two very obscure references in my research.

The Baking Powder is located in the Rosedale Mining District at the extreme north end of the San Mateo mountains in southern Socorro county, New Mexico. I have not examined the mining claim records in the local courthouse for exact dates (mainly because you are the very first individual to ever request information on the property!) but would predict the claim (or claims) was located during latter part of the 19th century -- poss. mid-1890s -- as a result of the success of the well-known Rosedale mine and discovery of the nearby White Cap.

The "veins" in the Rosedale district are actually brecciated shear zones in the volcanic (rhyolitic) rocks The brecciated and sheared rhyolite has been recemented with a hard, bluish-white quartz and later with a clearer vein-type quartz. The entire vein mass is highly silicified and in those areas yielding the best gold values are heavily stained with the black and red oxides of manganese and iron respectively. Gold occurred in the native state in the upper oxidized portions of the vein but is very nearly absent in the sulfide portion at or below the water table. Remarkably, little or no silver is present. I would predict the Baking Powder "vein" to be similar in character to the above. Dr. Charles Ferguson's doctoral dissertation covered a large area extending from the southern end of the Rosedale District to the north well beyond White Cap and Big Rosa canyons. I asked Charlie if he knew the locality of the Baking Powder and other prospects and he indicated approximate locations for two unnamed mine workings about two miles north and northwest of the Rosedale which I feel are the White Cap and the Baking Powder. The projected location for the latter is approx. Sec3, T6S, R6W near the head of Big Rosa canyon.

Soon after the turn of the century, development on the Baking Powder had apparently progressed to the mining stage. According to a note in the Engineering and Mining Journal, 24 December 1903, p 988, the Baking Powder mine was said to be initiating "full operations," whatever that meant; Walter Edwards, undoubtedly your ancestor, was the manager. Unfortunately the operation failed to live up to expectations and within four years was facing foreclosure for $1200 in back wages (Soccoro Chieftan, 30 November 1907). The obvious conclusion is that the mine failed to develop pay ore in sufficient quantities to sustain the operation and it failed. And that is the current extent of the "historic" record!

I and my colleagues attempted to visit this prospect in May 2000, but despite our "approximate" location on the topo sheet, and a full day's search, four-wheeling, etc., we failed to locate it. I should note that the 'road' up Big Rosa canyon is, in places, a figment of the imagination -- we could have easily missed a small prospect off in the ponderosas! The Mount Whithington jeep road may pass within a mile of the mine on the west and that is the route I will next attempt.

Now that you have made a request for information, I shall keep a sharp lookout for additional data. I must yet peruse the pages of the few issues of the San Marcial Bee that have survived the ravages of time and will keep you in mind should anything materialize. Additionally I will examine the claim location records upon my next visit to the courthouse. On the other hand, I'd be most pleased to add to our archival files any information you'd be willing to share with us from your family's papers. Regards,

Robert W. Eveleth Senior
Mining Engineer Curator,
Mining Archives

Dear Mr. Edwards:

Recent research on several articles of local mining interest has, once again, led me through the pages of the Socorro Chieftain. Recalling your interest in the above, I made a copy of an article on the Baking Powder/Edwards Bros., reproduced below in its entirety:

Socorro Chieftain, 6/14/1902, p 4: "Rosedale, N. M., June 10m, 1902 -- Editor

Chieftain -- Rosedale is quiet at present. Big Rosa, 2-1/2 miles to the northwest, shows great and rapidly increasing activity. Fully $5,000 worth of work is now underway and other contracts are being let. The immediate cause of this work was the discovery and partial development of the Baking Powder property of the Edwards Brothers of El Paso, Tex. This claim showed well from the surface but now at a depth of 55 feet it is exciting old time prospectors and tenderfeet alike by yielding a strong vein of high grade ore while picked samples show as high as 84 ounces in gold. Two or more stamp mills, stores, drink emporiums, a post office, dozens of cabins and tents, a good graded road up Big Rosa, and a couple of hundred men tearing into its mountain sides may be a vision, but as a miner and prospector of long experience I think this and more will be a reality within 12 months. Big Rosa may not be as good a mining camp as Cripple Creek, Colo. It may be better. The writer has no interest there and is not puffing the camp to "induce capital," but is sincere in saying that right now is a suitable and very favorable time to investigate Big Rosa.

There can be no harm in keeping an eye on the indicator." Signed: A. L. Heister."

As I continue to go through the pages of the Socorro Chieftan, I'll be sure to let you know if the writer's dream materialized.

Best Regards,
Robert W. Eveleth
Senior Mining Engineer

----

26.   iii. AMBROSE EDWIN EDWARDS was born on 20 Mar 1872 in Sulphur Springs, Texas. He died on 15 Feb 1963 in Dallas, Texas. He married Anne Buntin Yarbrough, daughter of George Yarbrough and Margaret Augusta Herrin on 03 Jul 1901 in Grayson County, Texas. She was born on 15 Oct 1871 in Tyler, Texas. She died on 24 Oct 1955 in Dallas, Texas.

    v. MARVIN M. EDWARDS was born on 28 Nov 1875 in Riley Springs, Texas. He died on 11 Sep 1900 in Strawn, Texas.

More About Marvin M. Edwards:
Burial: Mount Marion Cemetery, Strawn, Texas
Cause Of Death: Consumption (Tuberculosis)
Living In: 1900 Palo Pinto County, Texas with his parents

27.   v. MCDONALD EDWARDS was born on 10 Dec 1877 in Strawn, Texas. He died on 08 Nov 1957 in Lubbock, Texas. He married Sally May Marchbanks, daughter of Finley W. Marchbanks and Sarah A. Hix on 26 Feb 1899 in Strawn, Texas. She was born on 12 Feb 1877 in Cleburne, Texas. She died on 27 Oct 1957 in Fort Worth, Texas.

28.   vi. LEROY ARDIS EDWARDS was born on 27 Feb 1881 in Sulphur Springs, Texas. He died on 05 Dec 1951 in Loraine, Texas. He married (1) EMMA GEORGIE IRENE GARLAND, daughter of Edward Warren Garland and Julia Rebecca Kimbell on 27 Jul 1921 in Roscoe, Texas. She was born on 23 Mar 1880 in Annona, Texas. She died on 17 Dec 1969 in Kerrville, Texas. He married (2) ADA MAY LOFLIN, daughter of Daniel Vance Loflin and Margarite Sophia Crawley on 21 Nov 1906 in Palo Pinto County, Texas. She was born on 26 Apr 1886 in Palo Pinto County, Texas. She died on 15 Apr 1918 in Loraine, Texas.

29.   vii. BECTON GOODSON EDWARDS was born on 29 Oct 1884 in Sulphur Springs, Texas.

He died on 04 Dec 1960 in Dallas, Dallas County, Texas. He married Minnie Mae Strain, daughter of George Douglas Strain and Sarah Elizabeth Strawn on 04 Nov 1908 in Weatherford, Texas. She was born on 22 Feb 1887 in Strawn, Texas. She died on 28 Jul 1956 in Corsicana, Navarro County, Texas.

    viii.   JOHN MCTYEIRE EDWARDS was born on 08 Dec 1888 in Eliasville, Texas. He died on 05 Oct 1970 in Killeen, Texas.

More About John McTyeire Edwards:
Burial: 09 Oct 1970 in Fort Sam Houston National Cemetery, San Antonio, Texas Cause Of Death: Acute Myocardial Infarction, Generalized Arteriosclerosis
Living In: 1910 Greenville, Texas
Occupation: 1920 in Palo Pinto County, Texas; Bank Cashier
Occupation: 1930 in San Antonio, Texas; Hotel Clerk
Occupation: 1940 in San Antonio, Texas; Private Residence Gardener
Military Service: Bet. 19 Sep 1917-24 Mar 1919; Sergeant First Class, World War One

Notes for John McTyeire
Edwards: Never Married

Probably named after John McTyeire of Russell County, Alabama.

Served in HQ Company, 165th Depot Brigade, U.S. Army

----

7.   CHARLES ANDERSON BROWN[2] EDWARDS (Ambrose[1]) was born on 25 Oct 1846 in Russell County, Alabama. He died on 23 Dec 1937 in Dothan, Alabama. He married Martha Caroline Crittenden, daughter of Cincinnatus Decatur Crittenden and Emeline Amanda Mahone on 01 Sep 1867 in Ozark, Alabama. She was born on 09 Feb 1851 in Schley County, Georgia. She died on 04 Apr 1929 in Ozark, Alabama.

More About Charles Anderson Brown Edwards:
Burial: 24 Dec 1937 in Morning View Cemetery, Ozark, Alabama
Occupation: 1870 in Dale County, Alabama; Farmer
Occupation: 1880 in Daleville, Dale County, Alabama; Farmer
Occupation: 1900 in Daleville, Dale County, Alabama; Farmer
Occupation: 1910 in Ozark, Alabama; Farmer
Occupation: Bet. 16 Jan 1911-16 Jan 1917 in Dale County, Alabama; Probate Judge
Occupation: 1920 in Ozark, Alabama; Retired
Occupation: 1930 in Ozark, Alabama; Retired
Military Service: Bef. Feb 1864; Company A., Goldson's Alabama Battalion
Military Service: Bet. Feb 1864-05 May 1865; Company A, Brown's Independant Cavalry, Davidson's Battalion, Alabama Cavalry
Property: 1870 in Dale County, Alabama; 100 Acres Improved and 230 Acres Unimproved

Notes for Charles Anderson Brown Edwards:
Served two terms in the Alabama state legislature from Dale County; 1887-1889 and 1890-1891.

Paroled May 5, 1865 at Eufaula, Alabama.

More About Martha Caroline Crittenden:

Burial: 05 Apr 1929 in Morning View Cemetery, Ozark, Alabama

Notes for Martha Caroline Crittenden:
"Caroline" is the spelling used in the 1860 U.S. census.

Charles Anderson Brown Edwards and Martha Caroline Crittenden had the following children:

30.   i. TULLY DECATUR LAMAR[3] EDWARDS was born on 28 Dec 1870 in Dale County, Alabama. He died on 06 Feb 1942 in Dothan, Houston County, Alabama. He married Claudia Blackman on 22 Feb 1894 in Ozark, Alabama. She was born in Jan 1873 in Alabama. She died on 23 Nov 1954 in Coffee County, Alabama.

31.   ii. EURA EMELINE AMANDA EDWARDS was born on 28 Nov 1871 in Dale County, Alabama. She died on 16 Apr 1960 in Ozark, Alabama. She married Joseph Harris Adams, son of Joseph A. Adams and Annie Laurie Kirksey on 11 Oct 1891 in Ozark, Alabama. He was born on 12 Aug 1870 in Newton, Dale County, Alabama. He died on 13 Jan 1918 in Houston County, Alabama.

        iii.   CHARLES M. EDWARDS was born on 11 Sep 1873 in Dale County, Alabama. He died on 30 Nov 1875 in Dale County, Alabama.

                More About Charles M. Edwards:
                Burial: Morning View Cemetery, Ozark, Alabama

32.   iv. LILLIAN VIRGINIA EDWARDS was born on 29 Jul 1876 in Dale County, Alabama. She died on 22 Jan 1914 in Enterprise, Alabama. She married Jackson Maryland Young, son of William Young and Mary Davenport on 24 Mar 1901 in Ozark, Alabama. He was born on 07 Jan 1873 in Pine Level, Alabama. He died on 11 Nov 1949 in St. Petersburg, Florida.

33.   v. RENA CAROLYN EDWARDS was born on 21 Jul 1878 in Dale County, Alabama. She died on 22 Oct 1978 in Talledega, Alabama. She married Clifford Malone Cox, son of Willis S. Cox and Hattie Wingate on 28 Apr 1900 in Ozark, Alabama. He was born on 17 Apr 1871 in Alabama. He died on 03 Feb 1932 in Dothan, Houston County, Alabama.

        vi.   CHARLES ANDERSON BROWN EDWARDS JR. was born on 24 Sep 1880 in Dale County, Alabama. He died on 09 May 1962 in Ozark, Alabama.

                More About Charles Anderson Brown Edwards Jr.:
                Burial: Morning View Cemetery, Ozark, Alabama
                Living In: 1910 Living with his parents in Ozark, Alabama
                Living In: 1920 Living with his parents in Ozark, Alabama.
                Living In: 1930 Living with his father in Ozark, Alabama
                Occupation: 1900 in Daleville, Dale County, Alabama; Teacher
                Occupation: 1910 in Ozark, Alabama; Dry Goods Salesman
                Occupation: 1920 in Ozark, Alabama; Overseer on Farm

34.   vii. HIRAM FLOURNOY EDWARDS was born on 14 Dec 1883 in Dale County, Alabama. He died on 25 Feb 1971 in Ozark, Dale County, Alabama. He married Lena Rebecca Johnson, daughter of Henry Johnson and Evie Sellers on 09 Jun 1912 in Enterprise, Alabama. She was born on 28 Sep 1894 in Ozark, Alabama. She died on 11 Nov 1971 in Ozark, Dale County, Alabama.

35. viii. WALTER LEROY EDWARDS was born on 14 Dec 1883 in Dale County, Alabama. He died on 08 Dec 1975 in Ozark, Alabama. He married Mary Tom Ray on 21 May 1912 in Ozark, Alabama. She was born on 31 Aug 1892 in Brundidge, Alabama. She died on 04 Nov 1967 in Ozark, Alabama.

36. ix. LUCILLE EDWARDS was born on 02 Jan 1890 in Dale County, Alabama. She died on 20 May 1969 in Geneva, Alabama. She married Frederick Malcolm Fleming, son of William Leroy Fleming and Mary Love Edwards on 24 Mar 1910 in Ozark, Alabama. He was born on 20 Jan 1888 in Brundidge, Alabama. He died on 09 Jan 1953 in Montgomery, Montgomery County, Alabama.

8. WALTER STARR[2] EDWARDS (Ambrose[1]) was born on 09 Sep 1850 in Russell County, Alabama. He died on 21 Sep 1927 in Geneva, Geneva County, Alabama. He married Sarah Frances Brown on 8 Jan 1871. She was born on 10 May 1853 in Georgia. She died on 30 May 1920 in Enterprise, Alabama.

More About Walter Starr Edwards:
Burial: Enterprise City Cemetery, Enterprise, Alabama
Occupation: 1870 in Westville, Dale County, Alabama; School Teacher
Occupation: 1880 in Westville, Dale County, Alabama; Farmer
Occupation: 1892; Superintendent of Education, Coffee County, Alabama. Elected August 1, 1892 and commissioned August 25, 1892.
Occupation: 1894 in Coffee County, Alabama; County Superintendant of Education. Elected August 6, 1894 and commisioned September 25, 1894.
Occupation: 1900 in Enterprise, Alabama; Timber Agent
Occupation: 1903 ; Notary Public, Enterprise, Alabama. Appointed February 28, 1903 and commissioned March 6, 1903.
Occupation: 1910 in Enterprise, Alabama; Life Insurance Agent
Occupation: 1920 in Enterprise, Alabama; City Clerk
Property: 1880 in Dale County, Alabama; 65 Acres Improved and 70 Acres Unimproved

Notes for Walter Starr Edwards:
Death record gives Geneva, Geneva County, Alabama as place of death.

More About Sarah Frances Brown:
Burial: Enterprise City Cemetery, Enterprise, Alabama

Walter Starr Edwards and Sarah Frances Brown had the following children:

37. i. WALTER A.[3] EDWARDS was born on 06 Nov 1871 in Coffee County, Alabama. He died on 14 May 1906 in Enterprise, Alabama. He married Rattie Clifford Warren, daughter of William Warren and Emeline Leslie Thompson about 1896. She was born in Apr 1872 in Alabama.

38. ii. LUDIE EDWARDS was born about 1876 in Alabama. She died on 02 Jul 1931 in Montgomery, Alabama. She married Frank Glenn Park, son of Frank Park and Anne (unknown) on 08 Dec 1898 in Enterprise, Alabama. He was born in Apr 1859 in Alabama. He died on 26 May 1909 in Enterprise, Alabama.

39. iii. HELENA AUGUSTA EDWARDS was born on 31 Aug 1878 in Alabama. She died on 24 Feb 1920 in Garrison, Geneva County, Alabama. She married Frank W. Enzor on 21 Nov 1897 in Coffee County, Alabama. He was born on 03 Jul 1877 in Alabama. He died on 26 Jan 1968 in Crestview, Florida.

40.   iv. LOUISA JAMES EDWARDS was born on 10 Dec 1880 in Alabama. She died on 17 Jul 1953 in Greenville, Alabama. She married Nat Woodruff Thornton on 20 Apr 1900 in Coffee County, Alabama. He was born on 23 Jun 1873 in Barbour County, Alabama. He died on 30 Dec 1947 in Dothan, Alabama.

41.   v. CHARLES BROWN EDWARDS was born on 01 Apr 1884 in Enterprise, Alabama. He died on 28 Jun 1956 in Houston, Texas. He married EMILY EULALIA RIGDEN. She was born on 15 Aug 1889 in Geneva, Alabama. She died on 04 Oct 1970 in Houston, Texas.

42.   vi. MACKEY MAUDE EDWARDS was born on 12 Jun 1887 in Alabama. She died on 23 Oct 1977 in Milton, Florida. She married WILLIAM BURIAN KILLEBREW. He was born on 18 Sep 1870 in Newton, Alabama. He died on 19 Nov 1946 in Galveston, Texas.

43.   vii. LOVELACE YOUNG EDWARDS was born on 01 May 1889 in Enterprise, Alabama. He died on 15 Oct 1952 in Houston, Texas. He married Clara Inez Ralston, daughter of Wilbur L. Ralston and Barbara Frances Wampler on 16 Oct 1918 in Glendale, Arizona. She was born on 15 Oct 1891 in Dalton, Wayne County, Ohio. She died on 25 Dec 1976 in Houston, Texas.

44.   viii. JOHNNIE EUDORA EDWARDS was born on 24 Feb 1892 in Enterprise, Alabama. She died in 1975 in Montgomery, Alabama. She married Angus Edwin Edwards, son of Robert Charles Edwards and Francesca La Coates on 20 Nov 1917 in Enterprise, Alabama. He was born on 07 Aug 1887 in Haw Ridge, Alabama. He died on 19 Mar 1966 in Montgomery, Alabama.

    ix. CUSTIS CECIL EDWARDS was born on 28 Mar 1896 in Alabama. He died on 22 Jun 1921 in Enterprise, Alabama.

More About Custis Cecil Edwards:
Burial: Enterprise City Cemetery, Enterprise, Alabama
Occupation: 1917 in Crenshaw County, Alabama; Distributes U.S. Mail
Occupation: 1920 in Enterprise, Alabama; Rural Mail Carrier

Generation 3

9.   **WILLIAM CAPERS**[3] **MIZELL** (Martha Louise[2] Edwards, Ambrose[1] Edwards) was born on 01 Oct 1844 in Russell County, Alabama. He died on 10 Sep 1934 in Ozark, Dale County, Alabama. He married Roxanna Chalker, daughter of William W. Chalker and Rebecca Anderson Land on 28 May 1871. She was born in 1848. She died on 27 Jan 1924 in Dothan, Houston County, Alabama.

More About William Capers Mizell:
Burial: 11 Sep 1934 in Union Cemetery, Ozark, Dale County, Alabama
Military Service: Bet. Jun 1861-Apr 1865; Company E, 15th Alabama Infantry, C.S.A.

Notes for William Capers Mizell:
Wounded at Spottsylvania, Chickamauga and Cold Harbor.
Engagements: Winchester, Cross Keys, Suffolk, Sharpsburg, Gettysburg, Battle Mount, Chickamauga, Fort Gilmer, Fort Harrison, Darbytown, Darbytown Road, Cedar Mountain, Spottsylvania, Cold Harbor, Shepardstown, Fredricksburg, Racoon Mountain, Lookout Valley, Camel Station, Knoxville, Dandridge, Chester Station, Deep Bottom, Fussell Mill, Appomattox.
Survived the War to surrender with his Company at Appomattox Court House. Pre War residence was at Westville, Alabama.

More About Roxanna Chalker:
Burial: Union Cemetery, Ozark, Dale County, Alabama

William Capers Mizell and Roxanna Chalker had the following children:

    i.   ROXANNE[4] MIZELL was born in 1872.

    ii.   AMELIA MIZELL was born in 1874.

    iii.   TODIE MIZELL was born in 1876. She married W. B. Goodbread on 20 Apr 1892 in Dale County, Alabama.

    iv.   MARY MIZELL was born in 1878.

    v.   WILLIAM MIZELL was born in 1880.

10.   **ELVIRA ARIANNA[3] MIZELL** (Martha Louise[2] Edwards, Ambrose[1] Edwards) was born on 31 Mar 1851 in Coffee County, Alabama. She died on 01 May 1940 in Johnson County, Texas. She married Alfred Ward Kennon, son of Isham Kennon and Elizabeth (unknown) on 09 Apr 1868 in Haw Ridge, Alabama. He was born on 08 Jul 1847 in Alabama. He died on 20 Nov 1922 in Texas.

More About Elvira Arianna Mizell:
Burial: Bono Cemetery, Johnson County, Texas

More About Alfred Ward Kennon:
Burial: Bono Cemetery, Johnson County, Texas

Alfred Ward Kennon and Elvira Arianna Mizell had the following children:

    i.   ADDIE LAURA[4] KENNON was born in Feb 1869 in Dale County, Alabama. She married WALTER M. HILLYER. He was born in 1860 in Mississippi.

    ii.   HENRY HOPE KENNON was born in Jun 1870 in Panola County, Texas. He married Fannie Bratcher on 03 Dec 1891 in Johnson County, Texas. She was born in Feb 1877 in Tennessee.

    iii.   JOHN WALTER KENNON was born on 31 Aug 1873 in Panola County, Texas. He died on 12 Nov 1952. He married Claudia May Templeton, daughter of (unknown) Templeton and Virginia Ana Long on 24 Dec 1899 in Johnson County, Texas. She was born on 14 Sep 1877 in Franklin County, Texas. She died on 18 Jul 1951.

    iv.   JULIUS ALFRED KENNON was born in Jan 1876 in Panola County, Texas. He married Daisy Baird about 1915. She was born about 1890 in Texas.

    v.   MATTIE MARTHA KENNON was born on 13 Jan 1879 in Ellis County, Texas. She died on 17 May 1906 in Texas. She married Ernest Rogers on 24 Dec 1900 in Johnson County, Texas.

    vi.   EVA KENNON was born in Sep 1883 in Ellis County, Texas. She married Leonard E. Davis on 19 Oct 1898. He was born in Mar 1870 in Texas.

    vii.   MITTIE LOVE KENNON was born in Apr 1886 in Texas. She died on 18 Jul 1979 in Tarrant County, Texas. She married JESS RAWLENCE.

viii. BERTTIE KENNON was born in Apr 1887 in Texas. She married Walter E. Rogers on 23 May 1901 in Johnson County, Texas.

ix. ISHAM GEORGE KENNON was born in Dec 1888 in Nemo, Texas. He died on 04 Aug 1979 in Tarrant County, Texas. He married ORA LEE WILLIAMSON. She was born on 6 Apr 1891 in Texas. She died in May 1985 in Tarrant County, Texas.

x. RUTH E. KENNON was born in Dec 1892 in Bono, Texas. She married GEORGE ODELL DORRIS.

11. **MARY LOVE**[3] **EDWARDS** (LeRoy Marion[2], Ambrose[1]) was born on 30 Dec 1851 in Russell County, Alabama. She died on 05 Jul 1934 in Brundidge, Alabama. She married William Leroy Fleming, son of John Alexander Fleming and Nancy Watson on 17 Jul 1873 in Dale County, Alabama. He was born on 19 Apr 1848 in Harris County, Georgia. He died on 20 Feb 1920 in Pike County, Alabama.

More About Mary Love Edwards:
b: 30 Dec 1851
Burial: Brundidge City Cemetery, Brundidge, Pike County, Alabama
Living In: 1930 Brundidge, Pike County, Alabama

More About William Leroy
Fleming: b: 19 Apr 1848
Burial: Brundidge City Cemetery, Brundidge, Pike County, Alabama
Living In: 1880 Pike County, Alabama
Occupation: 1880 in Grimes, Pike County, Alabama; Farmer
Occupation: 1900 in Dixon, Pike County, Alabama; Farmer
Occupation: 1910 in Pike County, Alabama; Farmer
Occupation: 1920 in Brundidge, Pike County, Alabama; Fuel and Lumber Dealer

Notes for William Leroy Fleming:
Justice of the Peace, Pike County, Alabama
State Legislature 1893-1895

William Leroy Fleming and Mary Love Edwards had the following children:

i. WALTER LYNWOOD[4] FLEMING was born on 08 Apr 1874 in Brundidge, Pike County, Alabama. He died on 03 Aug 1932 in Nashville, Tennessee. He married Mary Wright Boyd, daughter of David French Boyd and Esther G. Wright on 17 Sep 1902 in Auburn, Alabama. She was born about 1879 in Louisiana.

More About Walter Lynwood Fleming:
Living In: 1910 East Baton Rouge Louisiana
Living In: 1920 Nashville, Tennessee
Occupation: University Professor
Military Service: Spanish American War

Notes for Walter Lynwood Fleming:
Professor of History at West Virginia University 1903-1907.
Professor of History at Louisiana State University 1907-1917.
Head of the History and Political Science Department at Vanderbilt University 1917-1929.
First Sergeant, Company A, Alabama Volunteer Infantry.

2nd Lieutenant, Company H, 3rd Alabama Volunteer
Infantry. Elected to the Alabama Hall of Fame - 1957.

ii.   WILLIAM EDWARDS FLEMING was born on 27 Jun 1876 in Pike County, Alabama. He
      died on 03 Feb 1934 in Brundidge, Alabama. He married Elizabeth Anders on 10
      Dec 1899. She was born in Nov 1879 in Alabama. She died in 1964.

      More About William Edwards Fleming:
      Burial: Brundidge City Cemetery, Brundidge, Alabama

iii. EMELINE LOVE FLEMING was born on 29 Dec 1877 in Brundidge, Pike
      County, Alabama. She died on 27 Feb 1956 in Brundidge, Alabama.

      More About Emeline Love Fleming:
      Occupation: 1920; Teacher, Brundidge, Alabama

iv.   MARTHA LEE FLEMING was born in Mar 1879 in Brundidge, Pike County, Alabama.
      She died on 29 Mar 1948 in Geneva, Alabama. She married Conley P.
      McEachern about 1900. He was born in Jul 1871 in Alabama.

v.   MARY EVELYN FLEMING was born on 29 Jan 1881 in Brundidge, Pike
      County, Alabama. She died on 02 Jan 1963 in Troy, Alabama.

vi.   JOHN ALEXANDER FLEMING was born on 05 May 1882 in Pike County, Alabama. He
      died on 22 Aug 1884.

vii. LEROY MARION FLEMING was born on 27 Jan 1884 in Pike County, Alabama. He
      died in 1946. He married Lela Mae Hightower, daughter of Charles W.
      Hightower and Eugenia Deese about 1910. She was born on 05 May 1890 in
      Alabama. She died on 23 Jun 1990 in Blountsville, Alabama.

      More About Leroy Marion Fleming:
      Occupation: 1910; Merchant, Brundidge, Alabama
      Occupation: 1930; Lumber Dealer, Brundidge, Alabama

viii. FRANCES OLIVIA FLEMING was born on 14 Feb 1886 in Brundidge, Pike
      County, Alabama. She died about 1975.

      More About Frances Olivia Fleming:
      Occupation: 1920 ; Teacher, Brundidge, Alabama

ix.   FREDERICK MALCOLM FLEMING was born on 20 Jan 1888 in Brundidge, Alabama. He
      died on 09 Jan 1953 in Montgomery, Montgomery County, Alabama. He married
      Lucille Edwards, daughter of Charles Anderson Brown Edwards and Martha
      Caroline Crittenden on 24 Mar 1910 in Ozark, Alabama. She was born on 02 Jan
      1890 in Dale County, Alabama. She died on 20 May 1969 in Geneva, Alabama.

      More About Frederick Malcolm Fleming:
      b: 20 Jan 1888 in Brundidge, Alabama
      Burial: Geneva City Cemetery, Geneva, Alabama

Occupation: 1910 in Enterprise, Alabama; City School Teacher
Occupation: 1917 in Geneva County, Alabama; Livestock Dealer
Occupation: 1920 in Geneva, Geneva County, Alabama; Livestock Dealer
Occupation: 1930 in Geneva, Geneva County, Alabama; Building Contractor
Military Service: 1925 in Geneva County, Alabama; Captain in Battery E,
141st Field Artillery, Alabama National Guard

12. ARCHIBALD GAULDING[3] EDWARDS (LeRoy Marion[2], Ambrose[1]) was born on 01 May 1854 in Dale County, Alabama. He died on 08 Oct 1903 in Enterprise, Alabama. He married Virginia Leonard Crittenden, daughter of Cincinnatus Decatur Crittenden and Emeline Amanda Mahone about 1876. She was born on 03 Oct 1857 in Georgia. She died on 11 Oct 1902 in Enterprise, Alabama.

More About Archibald Gaulding Edwards:
b: 1854
Burial: Enterprise City Cemetery, Enterprise, Alabama
Occupation: 1880 in Westville, Dale County, Alabama; Farmer
Occupation: 1900 in Daleville, Dale County, Alabama; Farmer

More About Virginia Leonard Crittenden:
b: 1857 in Georgia
Burial: Enterprise City Cemetery, Enterprise, Alabama

Archibald Gaulding Edwards and Virginia Leonard Crittenden had the following children:

i.   MARY L.[4] EDWARDS. She married D.M. TURNEY.

ii. CINCINNATUS FERNANDO EDWARDS was born on 19 Oct 1876 in Dale County, Alabama. He died on 08 Feb 1947 in Enterprise, Alabama. He married Dovie Adele Pridgen, daughter of Niram Stephen Pridgen and Angimiah Brock on 18 Jun 1896 in Dale County, Alabama. She was born on 27 Jan 1882 in Dale County, Alabama. She died on 26 Feb 1965 in Enterprise, Alabama.

     More About Cincinnatus Fernando Edwards:
     Burial: Enterprise City Cemetery, Enterprise,
     Alabama
     Cause Of Death: Cancer
     Occupation: Bet. 1902-1946; Retail Dry Goods Merchant, Enterprise,
     Alabama
     Occupation: Bet. 1908-1916; Mayor of Enterprise, Alabama

     Notes for Cincinnatus Fernando Edwards:
     Cinncinatus started working in his father's mercantile business In 1902. After his fathers death in 1903 Cinncinatus bought out the interests of the other heirs and ran the store until retiring in 1946.

iii. IDA LOVE EDWARDS was born in 1879 in Alabama. She died in 1926. She married JAMES BENJAMIN MARTIN. He was born in 1879. He died in 1968.

     More About Ida Love Edwards:
     Burial: Enterprise City Cemetery, Enterprise, Alabama

iv. MATTIE EDWARDS was born in Feb 1881 in Alabama.

v.   NANCY VIRGINIA EDWARDS was born on 05 Dec 1883 in Alabama. She died on 24 Jun 1957 in Alabama.

More About Nancy Virginia Edwards:
Burial: Enterprise City Cemetery, Enterprise, Alabama

vi. FLORENCE IRENE EDWARDS was born on 20 Jul 1886 in Alabama. She died on 30 Jan 1972 in Alabama.

More About Florence Irene Edwards:
Burial: Enterprise City Cemetery, Enterprise, Alabama

vii. ADDIE MARY EDWARDS was born on 11 Jan 1889 in Alabama. She died on 25 Mar 1974 in Alabama. She married VIRGIL O. WARREN. He was born on 01 Jul 1886. He died on 28 Apr 1963.

More About Addie Mary Edwards:
Burial: Enterprise City Cemetery, Enterprise, Alabama

viii. RENA LEE EDWARDS was born on 30 Jan 1892 in Alabama. She died on 04 Oct 1976 in Alabama.

More About Rena Lee Edwards:
Burial: Enterprise City Cemetery, Enterprise, Alabama

ix. LEILA FRANCES EDWARDS was born on 28 Feb 1894 in Alabama. She married James Stephen Pridgen, son of Niram Stephen Pridgen and Angimiah Brock on 04 Jan 1920 in Enterprise, Alabama. He was born in Dale County, Alabama.

x. WILLIAM A. EDWARDS was born in Sep 1896 in Alabama.

xi. MILLNER L. EDWARDS was born in May 1899 in Alabama.
xii.

13. **EMELINE AMBROSE[3] EDWARDS** (LeRoy Marion[2], Ambrose[1]) was born on 25 Jul 1855 in Dale County, Alabama. She died on 02 Jan 1933 in Shellman, Georgia. She married Joashley Fernando Crittenden, son of Cincinnatus Decatur Crittenden and Emeline Amanda Mahone about 1877. He was born on 03 Mar 1855 in Georgia. He died on 14 Jun 1929.

More About Emeline Ambrose Edwards:
Burial: Eastview City Cemetery, Shellman, Randolph County, Georgia

More About Joashley Fernando Crittenden:
Burial: Eastview City Cemetery, Shellman, Randolph County, Georgia
Occupation: 1880 in Randolph County, Georgia; Retail Merchant
Occupation: 1900 in Shellman, Georgia; Merchant
Occupation: 1910 in Randolph County, Georgia; Retail Merchant of General Merchandise
Occupation: 1920 in Shellman, Georgia; Retail Merchant

Joashley Fernando Crittenden and Emeline Ambrose Edwards had the following children:

i. ALBERT LEROY[4] CRITTENDEN was born on 02 Apr 1879 in Georgia. He died on 25 Jan 1934.

More About Albert LeRoy Crittenden:
Burial: Eastview City Cemetery, Shellman, Randolph County, Georgia

    ii.   LILLIAN CRITTENDEN was born in Sep 1881 in Georgia.

    iii.   INDIA B. CRITTENDEN was born in Jul 1884 in Georgia.

    iv.   WILLIAM R. CRITTENDEN was born on 09 Nov 1887 in Georgia. He died on 06 Dec 1937.

        More About William R. Crittenden:
        Burial: Eastview City Cemetery, Shellman, Randolph County, Georgia

    v.   MINNIE L. CRITTENDEN was born in Jul 1891 in Georgia.

    vi.   MARTHA F. CRITTENDEN was born in Dec 1892 in Georgia.

    vii. JOASHLEY C. CRITTENDEN was born in Sep 1895 in Georgia.

    viii. MALCOLM CRITTENDEN was born in Dec 1898 in Georgia. He married an unknown spouse about 1877.

14.   AMBROSE JOHN[3] EDWARDS (LeRoy Marion[2], Ambrose[1]) was born in Apr 1859 in Dale County, Alabama. He died on 25 Jan 1938 in Enterprise, Alabama. He married **MOENA BAMMA MATTHEWS**. She was born on 16 Nov 1858 in Dale County, Alabama. She died on 19 Mar 1915 in Enterprise, Alabama. He married **SARAH ANN CLARK**. She was born on 19 Apr 1875 in Alabama. She died on 29 May 1961 in Dothan, Alabama.

More About Ambrose John Edwards:
Burial: Enterprise City Cemetery, Enterprise, Alabama
Occupation: 1900 in Enterprise, Alabama; Farmer
Occupation: 1910 in Enterprise, Alabama; Retail Dry Goods Merchant

More About Moena Bamma Matthews:
Burial: Enterprise City Cemetery, Enterprise, Alabama

Ambrose John Edwards and Moena Bamma Matthews had the following children:

    i.   MATTIE E.[4] EDWARDS was born in Nov 1880 in Alabama.

    ii.   BAMMA MATTHEWS EDWARDS was born in Dec 1882 in Alabama. She died on 03 Feb 1967 in Montgomery, Alabama.

    iii.   JOHN AMBROSE EDWARDS was born on 10 Mar 1886 in Alabama. He died on 28 Jun 1907 in Enterprise, Alabama.

        More About John Ambrose Edwards:
        Burial: Enterprise City Cemetery, Enterprise, Alabama

    iv.   EMMIE L. EDWARDS was born in Mar 1888 in Alabama.

    v.   WILLIAM EDWARDS was born on 12 Oct 1889 in Alabama. He died on 22 Aug 1890.

More About William Edwards:
Burial: Pleasant Hill Methodist Cemetery, Ozark, Alabama

Notes for William Edwards:
Originally buried in Pleasant Hill Cemetery near Westville and moved to present Pleasant Hill Cemetery when Fort Rucker was established.

More About Sarah Ann Clark:
Burial: Enterprise City Cemetery, Enterprise, Alabama

15.   **LEROY MANSFIELD**[3] **EDWARDS** (LeRoy Marion[2], Ambrose[1]) was born on 21 Oct 1870 in Dale County, Alabama. He died in 1957. He married Charlotte Jane Morgan, daughter of George Morgan and Rebecca Hall on 04 Feb 1893 in Dale County, Alabama. She was born in Apr 1870 in Alabama. She died on 05 Feb 1945 in Brewton, Escambia County, Alabama.

More About LeRoy Mansfield Edwards:
Occupation: 1900 in Westville, Alabama; Farmer
Occupation: 1910 in Precinct 18, Coffee County, Alabama; Farmer
Occupation: 1920 in Bagdad, Sana Rosa County, Florida; Farmer
Occupation: 1930 in Brewton, Escambia County, Alabama; Farmer

Notes for LeRoy Mansfield Edwards:
1900 U.S. census gives birth date as October 1870.

LeRoy Mansfield Edwards and Charlotte Jane Morgan had the following children:

    i.   GEORGE[4] EDWARDS was born in Feb 1894 in Dale County, Alabama.

    ii.   VERA EDWARDS was born in Sep 1895 in Dale County, Alabama.

    iii.   WILLEY EDWARDS was born in Jul 1897 in Dale County, Alabama.

    iv.   CLARA EDWARDS was born in Jun 1899 in Dale County, Alabama.

    v.   JULIAN EDWARDS was born about 1901 in Alabama.

    vi.   RALPH EDWARDS was born about 1903 in Alabama.

    vii.   EUNICE EDWARDS was born about 1905 in Alabama.

    viii.   WALTER M. EDWARDS was born about 1909 in Alabama.

    ix.   LILLY BELL EDWARDS was born about 1909 in Alabama.

16.   **THEOPHILUS AMBROSE**[3] **EDWARDS** (William Archibald[2], Ambrose[1]) was born on 17 Jul 1859 in Dale County, Alabama. He died on 11 Feb 1929 in Dallas, Texas. He married Nora Elizabeth Bumpass, daughter of William Presley Bumpass and Mariah Hungerford Thomas on 26 Dec 1882 in Collin County, Texas. She was born on 26 Sep 1858 in Sulphur Springs, Texas. She died on 19 Apr 1927 in Grand Prarie, Texas.

More About Theophilus Ambrose Edwards:
Burial: 13 Feb 1929 in Restland Memorial Park, Dallas, Texas
Cause Of Death: pneumonia
Occupation: 1900 in Ellis County, Texas; Cotton Broker
Occupation: 1910 in Dallas, Texas; Raw Cotton Exporter
Occupation: 1920 in Tarrant County, Texas; Farmer

More About Nora Elizabeth Bumpass:
Burial: Restland Memorial Park, Dallas, Texas

Theophilus Ambrose Edwards and Nora Elizabeth Bumpass had the following children:

i. CLARA LILLIAN[4] EDWARDS was born on 12 Feb 1884 in Farmersville, Texas. She died on 26 Oct 1973 in Ennis, Texas. She married Robert Roy Connally on 22 Sep 1904 in Waxahachie, Texas. He was born on 28 Sep 1881 in Ellis County, Texas.

More About Clara Lillian Edwards: Burial: Hillcrest, Texas

ii. LAURA LEE OLIA EDWARDS was born on 09 Aug 1886 in Nevada, Texas. She died on 31 May 1981. She married Robert Weldford Troth on 17 Oct 1911 in Dallas, Texas. He was born on 20 Mar 1880 in Zachary, Louisiana. He died on 02 Feb 1951.

iii. THEOPHILUS MARVIN EDWARDS was born on 05 Sep 1888 in Farmersville, Texas. He died on 13 May 1969 in Dallas, Texas. He married Georgia Mae Barksdale on 12 Sep 1911 in Waxahachie, Texas. She was born on 27 Apr 1889 in Beckville, Texas. She died on 13 Apr 1986 in Dallas, Texas.

More About Theophilus Marvin Edwards:
Burial: 15 May 1969 in Restland Memorial Park, Dallas, Texas
Cause Of Death; Cerebral Thrombosis
Living In: 1942 Bryson, Texas
Occupation: Realty Investor

iv. RUBY ELIZABETH EDWARDS was born on 15 Nov 1893 in Waxahachie, Texas. She died on 24 Sep 1966 in Dallas, Texas. She married Luther Price Robertson on 06 Oct 1924 in Arlington, Texas. He was born on 10 Oct 1893. He died on 25 Dec 1971.

17. **MARY JAMES CORA[3] EDWARDS** (William Archibald[2], Ambrose[1]) was born on 06 Sep 1864 in Dale County, Alabama. She died on 15 Jul 1935 in Bella Vista, Arkansas. She married James Arthur Skillern, son of William Franklin Skillern and Sarah Ann Henninger on 04 Nov 1884 in Lewisville, Texas. He was born on 29 May 1856 in Pikeville, Tennessee. He died on 29 Dec 1914 in Dallas, Texas.

More About Mary James Cora Edwards:
Burial: Oak Cliff Cemetery, Dallas, Texas

More About James Arthur Skillern:
Burial: 30 Dec 1914 in Oak Cliff Cemetery, Dallas, Texas
Cause Of Death: ; Cancer
Living In: 1900 Oak Cliff, Dallas County, Texas
Living In: 1910 Dallas, Dallas County, Texas
Occupation: 1880 in Denton County, Texas; Drug Store Clerk

Occupation: 1896 in Dallas, Texas; Founded Skillern Drug Store Chain with first Dallas Store.

James Arthur Skillern and Mary James Cora Edwards had the following children:

i. WILLIAM ARTHUR[4] SKILLERN was born on 05 Aug 1885 in Lewisville, Texas. He died on 10 Jan 1922 in Dallas, Texas. He married Verna Lee Malone on 18 Jun 1907 in Dallas, Texas. She died on 20 Jul 1980.

More About William Arthur Skillern:
Burial: 11 Jan 1922 in Oak Cliff Cemetery, Dallas, Texas
Occupation: Druggist

ii. FRANK LLOYD SKILLERN was born on 05 Aug 1886 in Lewisville, Texas. He died on 26 Jan 1917 in Dallas, Texas. He married Elizabeth Peyton on 01 Oct 1908. She was born about 1889 in Texas.

More About Frank Lloyd Skillern:
Burial: 28 Jan 1917 in Oak Cliff Cemetery, Dallas, Texas
Occupation: 1910; Merchant, Dallas, Texas
Occupation: Druggist

Notes for Frank Lloyd Skillern:
Death Certificate gives August 24, 1886 as date of Birth.

iii. EDNA CORA SKILLERN was born on 31 Oct 1887 in Lewisville, Texas. She died on 21 Dec 1962 in Dallas, Texas. She married William Frank Cofer, son of Peter Joseph Cofer and Paulina Sawyer on 16 Apr 1912 in Dallas, Texas. He was born on 10 Mar 1884 in Illinois. He died on 13 Dec 1964 in Dallas, Dallas County, Texas.

More About Edna Cora Skillern:
Burial: 22 Dec 1962 in Laurel Land Cemetery, Dallas, Texas

iv. LIDA SKILLERN was born on 15 Aug 1889 in Lewisville, Texas. She died on 29 Aug 1971 in Dallas, Texas. She married (1) CHARLES BASCOM PETERSON on 11 Apr 1911 in Dallas, Texas. She married C. K. CONE.

More About Lida Skillern:
Burial: 30 Aug 1971 in Oak Cliff Cemetery, Dallas, Texas
Cause Of Death: Acute and Progressive CVA

v. RAE EDWARDS SKILLERN was born on 01 Nov 1894 in Sherman, Texas. He died on 15 Aug 1964 in Denton, Texas. He married Anne Wilson on 19 Nov 1913 in Dallas, Texas. She was born in 1894. She died on 15 Aug 1964.

More About Rae Edwards Skillern:
Burial: 15 Aug 1964 in Hillcrest Mausoleum, Dallas, Texas
Cause Of Death: Fractured Skull from Automobile-Truck Accident
Occupation: President of Skillern and Son.

vi. ZULA SKILLERN was born on 27 Aug 1899 in Dallas, Texas. She died on 16 Sep 1983 in Dallas, Texas. She married John Vest Folsom, son of Samuel Christopher

Folsom and Agnes Ann Traller on 11 Mar 1920 in Dallas, Texas. He was born on 11 Nov 1898 in Coryell County, Texas. He died on 18 Nov 1976.

Notes for Zula Skillern:
Zula Skillern And John Vest Folsom

John Vest Folsom was born in Coryell County on November 11, 1898 to Agnes Ann Traller and Samuel Christopher Folsom. Samuel, the son of Nancy Cobb and Elias Folsom, was born in Georgia in 1857. Agnes, the daughter of Sara Stevenson and Joseph H. Traller, was born in Gatesville on July 5, 1869. Her father was born at sea on November 16, 1832 to German emigrants en route to America. Her mother was born on August 19, 1842 in Arkansas to Emily Jane and James Hall Stevenson.

Zula Skillern was born in Dallas County on August 29, 1899 to Mamie Jane Edwards and James Arthur Skillern. Mamie was born in Dale County, Alabama on September 6, 1864 to Elizabeth Jane White and William A. Edwards, both natives of Georgia. James was born in Bledsoe County, Tennessee on May 29, 1856 to Sarah and William Skillern. His earliest ancestor in America was William Skillern, born in Ireland about 1710. Mamie and James were married in 1884 in Denton County. He died in 1914 and she in 1935, and both are buried in the Oak Cliff Cemetery in Dallas.

Zula?s father, James Skillern, was in Lewisville by 1880, where he established a drug store in 1885. By 1910 the company was known as ?Skillern and Sons Drugs? and had numerous stores throughout north Texas, with headquarters in Dallas. Her grandfather, William A. Edwards, was a prominent Methodist minister and a captain in the Confederate army. Between 1886 and 1900 Reverend Edwards served as pastor of many north Texas churches, in-cluding Cochran Chapel, East Dallas, West Dallas, and Haskell Avenue Methodist.

Samuel Folsom, father of John Vest, was a prominent farmer in Coryell County, who died in 1920 and is buried in the Mount Cemetery in Coryell County.

During World War I, J.V. was stationed with the army at Love Field and he remained in Dallas the rest of his life. On March 20, 1920 he and Zula were married. Zula had graduated from Oak Cliff High School and attended SMU and was active in a number of charitable, social, and women?s organizations in Dallas. Both Zula and J.V. were very active in the Oak Cliff Methodist Church and J.V. served as a leader of the North Texas Conference of the United Methodist Church and also as president of the Methodist Hospital Board.

J.V. worked with his brothers in Dallas during the 1920s and thirties at the Folsom Company, manufacturing attic fans and space heaters. The company also represented small national manufacturers as sales representatives in the southwest. In 1940 the organization was divided into two separate companies: brother Al took the manufacturing business and J.V. took the sales represen-tative business. J.V. founded the J.V. Folsom Company, a manufacturer?s representative company for housewares and garden equipment.

J.V. died on November 18, 1976 and Zula died on September 16, 1983. Both are entombed in the Hillcrest Mausoleum.

J.V. and Zula had two sons, John, Jr. and Robert Skillern. J.V., Jr. was born on July 20, 1924 and attended SMU. He was a pilot in the U.S. Army Air Corps and died in December 1944 while serving in the Pacific area during World War II.

Robert Skillern was born in Dallas on February 15, 1927. He graduated from Sunset High School and attended the U.S. Military Academy at West Point near the end of World War II. He graduated in 1949 from SMU with a Bachelor of Business Administration degree and was a member of Kappa Alpha Order. Active in athletics, he lettered in football, basketball, baseball, and track.

Bob worked as a sales representa-tive for the J.V. Folsom Company, but soon began real estate activity parttime. By 1954 real estate was a full-time job. He be-came a major developer of shop-ping centers, office buildings, apartments, individual areas, and residential subdivisions. His interest in golf led him to build Bent Tree and Gleneagles Country Clubs.

Bob Folsom served on the boards of many civic and charitable organizations, including the Cotton Bowl Association, the D/FW Airport, Methodist Hospital, and SMU. He was mayor of the City of Dallas from 1976 to 1981 and president of the Dallas Independent School District Board from 1964 to 1966. He was president of many organizations including Preston Trail Golf Club 1985, 1993-1994; Dallas Country Club, 1966; Texas Municipal League 1979-1980; and SMU Alumni Association 1971-1972.

He has received numerous awards for business and civic activities, including SMU Distinguished Alumnus in 1975, Headliner of the Year Dallas Press Club award in 1981, J. Eric Jonsson Aviation Award in 1990, SMU Lettermen?s Association Silver Anniversary Mustang Award in 1991, SMU Edwin Cox School of Business Distinguished Alumnus Award in 1995, and Award for Excellence in Hu-manities from the Dallas Histori-cal Society in 2000.

Robert married Margaret Monet Dalton on March 7, 1949 and they have four children. Margaret Diane was born May 14, 1950 and married first Wayne Miller and second Robert Frank. Debbie was born November 9, 1953 and married Don Michael Jarma. John Vest, III was born May 1, 1956 and died May 30, 1983. Robert Stephen was born January 2, 1959 and married Sharon Marie St. Germaine.

By Steve Folsom

vii.   ZOLA SKILLERN was born on 27 Aug 1899 in Dallas, Texas. She died on 01 Sep 1951 in Dallas, Texas. She married (1) WYLIE FONDREN WEATHERFORD, son of William Eugene Weatherford and Alta Mary Gable on 29 Jul 1922 in Ferris, Texas. He was born on 20 Dec 1894 in Texas. He died on 31 Mar 1951 in Tarrant County, Texas. She married (2) THOMAS CHAPMAN FERGUSON in Aug 1941. He was born on 18 Jul 1908 in Pennsylvania. He died on 16 Apr 1983 in Tarrant County, Texas.

     More About Zola Skillern:
     Burial: 03 Sep 1951 in Hillcrest Mausoleum, Dallas, Texas
     Cause Of Death: Liver Failure, Pneumonia and Cancer

viii.   MARY EVELYN SKILLERN was born on 15 Aug 1902 in Dallas, Texas. She died in Mar 1985 in Dallas, Texas. She married Leroy Monroe Napier, son of Leroy Munroe Napier on 10 Dec 1929. He was born on 19 Mar 1903. He died on 11 Jan 1969 in Dallas, Texas.

ix.   JEAN SKILLERN was born on 06 Dec 1906 in Dallas, Texas. She died on 17 Dec 1969. She married Robert Donald Hancock in 1932.

18. **A**NNIE **L**EE[3] **E**DWARDS (William Archibald[2], Ambrose[1]) was born on 08 Nov 1867 in Alabama. She died on 22 Apr 1908 in Haskell, Texas. She married Stephen Nathaniel Neathery, son of Allen Hill Neathery and Elizabeth Jemima Buie on 30 Dec 1884 in Denton County, Texas. He was born on 16 Jan 1864 in Texas. He died on 22 Nov 1943 in Haskell, Texas.

More About Annie Lee Edwards:
Burial: Willow Cemetery, Haskell, Haskell County, Texas

More About Stephen Nathaniel Neathery:
Burial: 22 Nov 1943 in Willow Cemetery, Haskell, Haskell County, Texas
Cause Of Death: Heart Attack
Occupation: 1900 in Farmersville, Texas; Cotton Broker
Occupation: 1910 in Haskell, Haskell County, Texas; Cotton Broker
Occupation: 1920 in Haskell, Haskell County, Texas; Cotton Broker
Occupation: 1930 in Haskell, Haskell County, Texas; Retired
Occupation: 1940 in Haskell, Haskell County, Texas; Retired

Notes for Stephen Nathaniel Neathery:
Death Certificate gives January 20, 1864 as date of birth.

Stephen Nathaniel Neathery and Annie Lee Edwards had the following children:

    i.   O**RPHIE** W**ILBUR**[4] N**EATHERY** was born on 17 Oct 1885 in Farmersville, Texas. He died on 03 May 1953 in Mangum, Oklahoma. He married Connie Wills in Apr 1909 in Wichita Falls, Texas. She was born on 26 Feb 1887. She died in Jun 1969 in San Antonio, Texas.

    ii.   V**ERA** I**ONE** N**EATHERY** was born on 23 Mar 1888 in Farmersville, Texas. She died on 15 Apr 1964 in Collin Coiunty, Texas. She married William Frederick Lampe on 17 Aug 1924. He was born on 27 Jul 1884 in Arlington, Texas. He died in Sep 1959 in Amarillo, Texas.

    iii.   F**AY** E**DWINA** N**EATHERY** was born on 05 Dec 1889 in Farmersville, Texas. She died on 06 Apr 1971 in Los Angeles, California. She married Wallace B. Alexander, son of Franklin Gates Alexander and Mary Melvina Henry on 15 Dec 1908 in Haskell County, Texas. He was born on 29 Oct 1888 in Haskell, Texas. He died in Dec 1964 in Ruidosa, New Mexico.

    iv.   D**ERON** A**DELLE** N**EATHERY** was born on 06 Apr 1892 in Farmersville, Texas. She died on 13 Aug 1972. She married John Richard Oates on 12 Apr 1911 in Haskell, Texas. He was born in Jan 1891 in Livingston, Texas. He died on 03 Dec 1965 in Tarrant County, Texas.

    v.   S**HIRLEY** L**ORENE** N**EATHERY** was born on 10 Mar 1893 in Farmersville, Texas. She died on 02 Jun 1980 in Fort Worth, Texas. She married Alexander Bruce Withers on 17 Aug 1914 in Dallas, Texas. He was born on 10 Aug 1891 in Mineral Wells, Texas.

        More About Shirley Lorene Neathery:
        Burial: Mineral Wells, Texas

    vi.   E**DWARD** A**LLEN** N**EATHERY** was born on 23 Feb 1900 in Farmersville, Texas. He died on 23 Sep 1971 in Dallas County, Texas. He married C**LARINE** W**ATSON**. She was born on 03 Feb 1904. She died on 12 Jan 1975 in Dallas, Texas.

Notes for Edward Allen Neathery:
Had no children.

vii.   BARNEY LEE NEATHERY was born on 24 Dec 1901 in Farmersville, Texas. He died on 12 Jul 1973 in Seymour, Texas. He married Gladys Edith England on 17 Mar 1927. She was born on 07 Apr 1903 in Commerce, Texas.

viii.

More About Barney Lee Neathery:
Occupation: 1920 in Haskell, Haskell County, Texas; Salesman at Drug Store

ix.   ELSA LUCILLE NEATHERY was born on 11 Apr 1904 in Farmersville, Texas. She died in Sep 1992. She married (1) WILLIAM RICHARD WEINERT in Haskell, Texas. He was born on 22 Mar 1900 in Sequin, Texas. He died on 03 May 1944 in San Antonio, Texas. She married RUFUS W. MAJORS. He was born on 17 Jul 1895. He died on 07 Jun 1968.

19.   **WILLIE MAUD**[3] **EDWARDS** (William Archibald[2], Ambrose[1]) was born on 22 Aug 1868 in Autauga County, Alabama. She died on 04 Aug 1946 in Dallas, Texas. She married Thomas Benton Lester on 03 Dec 1886 in Caddo, Indian Territory (Oklahoma). He was born on 29 Feb 1856 in Mississippi. He died on 13 Apr 1928 in Dallas, Texas.

More About Willie Maud Edwards:
Burial: 05 Aug 1946 in Oak Cliff Cemetery, Dallas,
Texas
Cause Of Death: Carcinoma of Breast
Occupation: 1910 in Dallas County, Texas; Working at dairy with her
husband
Occupation: 1920 in Dallas, Dallas County, Texas; Seamstress
Occupation: 1930 in Dallas, Dallas County, Texas; Proprietor of Retail Grocery

More About Thomas Benton Lester:
Burial: 14 Apr 1928 in Oak Cliff Cemetery, Dallas,
Texas
Cause Of Death: Bronchial Pneumonia
Occupation: 1880 in Denton County, Texas; Farm
Laborer
Occupation: 1900 in Dallas County, Texas; Manager
Occupation: 1910 in Dallas County, Texas; Dairy
Manager
Occupation: 1920 in Dallas, Dallas County, Texas; None

Thomas Benton Lester and Willie Maud Edwards had the following children:

i.   EULA AGNES[4] LESTER was born on 24 Aug 1887. She died on 19 Oct 1887.

ii.   MARY LEE LESTER was born on 19 Aug 1888 in Old Alton, Texas. She died in Jan 1891.

iii.   WILLIE ELIZA LESTER was born on 25 Sep 1890 in Denton, Texas. She died in 1983. She married C. B. Smith on 24 Sep 1911.

iv.   LOIS LESTER was born on 16 Aug 1892 in Lewisville, Texas. She died in Jul 1894.

v.   MAUDE LESTER was born on 08 Feb 1894 in Old Alton, Texas. She died on 28 Jan 1969. She married John Murrell in 1912.

More About Maude Lester:
Burial: Oak Cliff Cemetery, Dallas, Texas

vi.   BRYAN LEWIS LESTER was born on 04 Apr 1896 in Dallas County, Texas. He died on 10 Jul 1952. He married Eula Morris on 17 Sep 1914.

vii. WILLIAM ARCHIBALD EDWARDS LESTER was born on 31 Jul 1898 in Dallas County, Texas. He married Rose Brennon in Jan 1921.

More About William Archibald Edwards Lester:
Occupation: 1920 in Dallas, Dallas County, Texas; Switchboard Operator at Telephone Company.

viii. DOROTHY LESTER was born on 14 Feb 1900 in Dallas County, Texas. She died on 16 Jun 1924 in Dallas, Texas. She married Charles Clarence Carter in Nov 1918. He was born on 11 Apr 1900 in Terrell, Texas. He died on 04 Jun 1972 in Oregon.

More About Dorothy Lester:
Burial: 17 Jun 1924 in Oak Cliff Cemetery, Dallas, Texas
Cause Of Death: Complications of Childbirth

ix.   GLADYS LESTER was born on 10 Mar 1902. She died on 16 Jan 1903.

x.   TOMMIE LESTER was born on 11 Jul 1905 in Dallas County, Texas. She died on 16 Apr 1986 in Harris County, Texas. She married David McMinn Belt, son of David Belt and Alice Langston on 19 Oct 1924. He was born on 02 Jun 1899 in Waxahachie, Ellis County, Texas. He died on 05 May 1943 in Dallas, Dallas County, Texas.

More About Tommie Lester:
Living In: 1930   Divorced and living with her mother in Dallas, Texas
Occupation: 1930 in Dallas, Dallas County, Texas; Stenographer

20.   CARRIE LOUISE[3] EDWARDS (William Archibald[2], Ambrose[1]) was born on 30 Sep 1871 in Autaugaville, Alabama. She died on 25 Nov 1971 in Albuquerque, New Mexico. She married James Lee Wilson, son of William Henry Wilson and Elizabeth C. Pickens on 27 Feb 1889 in Mt. Pleasant, Texas. He was born on 09 Mar 1863 in Franklin, Holmes County, Mississippi. He died on 23 Jan 1917 in Celina, Collin County, Texas.

More About Carrie Louise Edwards:
Burial: 27 Nov 1971 in West Hill Cemetery, Grayson County, Texas
Occupation: 1920 in Celina, Collin County, Texas; Post Mistress
Occupation: 1930 in Wichita Falls, Texas; Teacher at Private School
Occupation: 1940 in Wichita Falls, Texas; None

More About James Lee Wilson:
Burial: West Hill Cemetery, Grayson County, Texas
Occupation: 1900 in Sherman, Texas; Editor
Occupation: 1910 in Collinsville, Texas; Newspaper Editor
Occupation: 1917 in Celina, Texas; Postmaster
Occupation: Newspaper Owner and Editor

Notes for James Lee Wilson:
Death certificate has March 6, 1863 for date of birth.

James Lee Wilson and Carrie Louise Edwards had the following children:
>   i. WILLIAM HENRY [4] WILSON was born on 13 Dec 1889 in McKinney, Texas. He died on 26 Apr 1959 in Dallas, Texas. He married EVELYN STORM. She was born in Quitman, Texas.
>
>   More About William Henry Wilson:
>   Burial: Restland Memorial Park, Dallas, Texas
>   Occupation: 1910 in Collinsville, Texas; Newspaper Printer
>   Occupation: Lawyer
>
>   ii. DOROTHY WILSON.
>
>   iii. ARIZONA WILSON was born on 29 Aug 1891 in Phoenix, Arizona. She died on 07 Apr 1977 in Little Rock, Arkansas. She married John Wesley Jackson on 24 Aug 1924.
>
>   More About Arizona Wilson:
>   Burial: Fairview Memorial Park, Albuquerque, New Mexico
>
>   iv. BENJAMIN LEE JONES WILSON was born on 18 Jul 1893 in Sherman, Texas.
>
>   Notes for Benjamin Lee Jones Wilson: Died in infancy.
>
>   v. MATTILYN WILSON was born on 17 Aug 1898 in Sherman, Texas.

21. **MATTIE ELIZABETH** [3] **EDWARDS** (William Archibald[2], Ambrose[1]) was born on 30 Sep 1871 in Autaugaville, Alabama. She died on 15 Oct 1969 in Dallas, Texas. She married Benjamin Lee Jones, son of William Edwards Jones and Lonette Holcombe on 27 Feb 1889 in Mt. Pleasant, Texas. He was born on 18 Mar 1862 in Collinsville, Texas. He died on 17 Sep 1937 in Dallas, Texas.

More About Mattie Elizabeth Edwards: Burial:
Hillcrest Memorial Park, Dallas, Texas Cause
Of Death: Cerebral Thrombosis

More About Benjamin Lee Jones:
Burial: Hillcrest Memorial Park, Dallas, Texas
Cause Of Death: Occlusion Of Coronary Artery
Occupation: 1895; Admitted to the Texas Bar.
Occupation: 1900 in Sherman, Texas; Lawyer
Occupation: Bet. Jan 1904-Jan 1912; District judge of the 15th Judicial District.
Occupation: 1910 in Sherman, Texas; Lawyer
Occupation: 1920 in Sherman, Texas; Lawyer
Occupation: 1930 in Dallas, Dallas County, Texas; Lawyer andJudge of Appeals Court
Occupation: 1937 in Dallas, Dallas County, Texas; Chief Justice of Court of Criminal Appeals

Benjamin Lee Jones and Mattie Elizabeth Edwards had the following children:
>   i. CARRIE WINIFRED [4] JONES was born on 15 Nov 1889 in Van Alstyne, Texas. She died

on 08 Sep 1977. She married Clarence Hugh McDaniel, son of E. M. McDaniel and Sophia Fulton on 16 Oct 1920 in Sherman, Texas. He was born on 29 Oct 1892 in Birmingham, Alabama. He died on 07 Apr 1970.

More About Carrie Winifred Jones:
Burial: Brownwood, Texas
Occupation: 1910 in Sherman, Texas; School Teacher

  ii. CHARLES EDWARDS JONES was born on 28 Jan 1891 in Dallas, Texas. He died on 2 Feb 1891.

  iii. LAURA GLADYS JONES was born on 16 Jan 1893 in Dallas, Texas. She died on 24 May 1894.

  iv. JAMES WILLIAM JONES was born on 05 Oct 1894 in Whitesboro, Texas. He died on 3 Feb 1981 in Dallas, Texas. He married Charlotte Ellen LeMay on 21 Apr 1915 in Dallas, Texas. She was born on 12 Jan 1895 in Mahtowa, Minnesota.
4
More About James William Jones:
Occupation: 1920 in Sherman, Texas; Military School Instructor

  v. BENJAMIN LEE JONES was born on 01 Oct 1900 in Sherman, Texas.

  vi. MARJORY RUTH JONES was born on 13 Apr 1904 in Sherman, Texas. She died on 18 Oct 1998 in Brown County, Texas. She married CHARLES CRAIG WOODSON. He was born on 06 Aug 1898 in Searcy, Arkansas. He died on 23 May 1971.

  vii. ROBERT WINTON JONES was born on 14 Jul 1906 in Sherman, Texas. He married LILLIAN AMELIA HANEY. She was born on 19 Jul 1904 in Dallas, Texas.

More About Robert Winton Jones:
Occupation: 1930 in Dallas, Dallas County, Texas; General Accountant
Occupation: C.P.A. , Freeport Sulphur Company

22. **ELIZA EMELINE[3] EDWARDS** (William Archibald[2], Ambrose[1]) was born on 09 Sep 1874 in Summerfield, Alabama. She died on 20 Jan 1964 in Dallas, Texas. She married George Henry Cochran, son of James Monroe Cochran and Margaret Lively on 30 Oct 1895 in Dallas, Texas. He was born on 04 Oct 1870 in Dallas, Texas. He died on 05 Apr 1956 in Dallas, Texas.

More About Eliza Emeline Edwards:
Burial: 22 Jan 1964 in Cochran Chapel Cemetery, Dallas, Texas
Cause Of Death: Cerebral Thrombosis

More About George Henry Cochran:
Burial: 06 Apr 1956 in Cochran Chapel Cemetery, Dallas, Texas
Cause Of Death: Pneumonia
Occupation: 1900 in Dallas County, Texas; Farmer
Occupation: 1910 in Dallas County, Texas; Farmer
Occupation: 1920 in Dallas, Dallas County, Texas; Vice President of Skillern Drug Store Chain, Dallas, Texas
Occupation: 1930 in Dallas, Dallas County, Texas; Vice President of Skillern Drug Store Chain,

Dallas, Texas

Notes for George Henry Cochran:
Headstone has October 4, 1870 for date of birth. Death certificate has October 2, 1870 for date of birth.

George Henry Cochran and Eliza Emeline Edwards had the following children:

    i.   MARGARET ELIZABETH[4] COCHRAN was born on 23 Nov 1901 in Dallas, Texas.

        More About Margaret Elizabeth Cochran:
        Living In: 1930 Living with her parents in Dallas, Texas.
        Occupation: 1930 in Dallas, Dallas County, Texas; Public School Teacher

    ii.   NELL COCHRAN was born about 1908.

        More About Nell Cochran:
        Living In: 1930 Living with her parents in Dallas, Texas.
        Occupation: 1930 in Dallas, Dallas County, Texas; Public School Teacher

23.   **AMBROSE PATRICK**[3] **WHITE** (Mary Clementine[2] Edwards, Ambrose[1] Edwards) was born on 15 Apr 1863 in Westville, Alabama. He died on 04 Jan 1933 in Ozark, Alabama. He married Henrietta Anderson Chalker, daughter of William W. Chalker and Rebecca Anderson Land on 06 Jan 1886 in Westville, Alabama. She was born on 11 Jan 1860 in Westville, Alabama. She died on 04 May 1943 in Ozark, Alabama.

More About Ambrose Patrick White:
Burial: Claybank Cemetery, Ozark, Dale County, Alabama
Occupation: 1880 in Daleville, Dale County, Alabama; Living and working on the farm of his uncle, C.A.B. Edwards.
Occupation: 1892 in Dale County, Alabama; Baliff of the Grand Jury
Occupation: 1900 in Ozark, Alabama; Broker
Occupation: 1910 in Ozark, Alabama; Occupation Unknown
Occupation: Bet. 1914-1919; Sheriff of Dale County, Alabama
Occupation: 1920 in Ozark, Alabama; Foreman at Fertilizer Factory
Occupation: Bet. 1923-1927; Sheriff of Dale County, Alabama
Occupation: 1930 in Ozark, Alabama; Farmer

More About Henrietta Anderson Chalker:
Burial: Claybank Cemetery, Ozark, Alabama

Ambrose Patrick White and Henrietta Anderson Chalker had the following children:

    i.   ANGUS PATRICK[4] WHITE was born on 26 Oct 1886 in Westville, Alabama. He died on 26 Apr 1933 in Ozark, Alabama. He married Annie Martha Smith, daughter of William Towns Smith and Missouri Wall on 29 Jan 1927 in Ariton, Alabama. She was born on 12 Jan 1902 in Ozark, Alabama. She died on 06 Apr 1989 in Ozark, Alabama.

        More About Angus Patrick White:
        Burial: Claybank Cemetery, Ozark, Dale County, Alabama
        Occupation: 1910 in Ozark, Alabama; Insurance Agent
        Occupation: 1920 in Ozark, Alabama; Insurance Agent

    ii.   CHARLES MORDECAI WHITE was born in Feb 1888 in Alabama. He married GRACE JAMES.

More About Charles Mordecai White:
Occupation: 1920 in Ozark, Alabama; Commercial Traveller for Hardware (Travelling Salesman)

    iii.   WALTER STRASS WHITE was born in Sep 1891. He married FRANCES LILLIAN MANN.

More About Walter Strass White:
Occupation: 1920 in Ozark, Alabama; Picture Show Manager

    iv.   LILLIAN REBECCA WHITE was born on 05 Jun 1898. She married HOMER JONES.

    v.   MARY ALPHONIA WHITE was born on 04 Aug 1900. She married Phocian Vines Hamrick in 1924.

More About Mary Alphonia White:
Occupation: 1920 in Ozark, Alabama; Picture Show Cashier

24.   THOMAS D.[3] WHITE (Mary Clementine[2] Edwards, Ambrose[1] Edwards) was born in Mar 1865 in Alabama. He married Emma Coleman in May 1890 in Greenwood, Florida. She was born in Feb 1864 in Ala bama.

More About Thomas D. White:
Living In: 1880 Westville, Dale County, Alabama with his uncle, Walter Starr Edwards.
Occupation: 1900 in Chipley, Washington County, Florida; Merchant
Occupation: 1910 in Chipley, Washington County, Florida; General Store Merchant
Occupation: 1920 in Chipley, Washington County, Florida; Hides and Furniture Dealer
Occupation: 1930 in Chipley, Washington County, Florida; Unknown Occupation and living as a boarder.

Thomas D. White and Emma Coleman had the following children:
    i.   THOMAS D.[4] WHITE was born in Mar 1891 in Florida.

More About Thomas D. White:
Occupation: 1910 in Chipley, Washington County, Florida; Salesman in his father's General Store.

    ii.   ETHEL WHITE was born in Feb 1893 in Florida.

    iii.   ROBERT C. WHITE was born in Feb 1897 in Florida.

    iv.   MARY WHITE was born about 1901 in Florida.

    v.   HARRY WHITE was born about 1904 in Florida.

25.   ISAAC MANSFIELD[3] EDWARDS (Ambrose Newton[2], Ambrose[1]) was born on 01 Feb 1868 in Strawn, Texas. He died on 18 Mar 1945 in Strawn Texas. He married Mary Sophronia (Onie) Strawn, daughter of Stephen Bethel Strawn and Emeline Jane Allen in 1899 in Palo Pinto County, Texas.

She was born on 11 Apr 1874 in Strawn, Texas. She died on 18 Feb 1950 in Temple, Bell
County, Texas.

More About Isaac Mansfield Edwards:
Burial: 19 Mar 1945 in Mount Marion Cemetery, Strawn, Texas
Cause Of Death: Coronary Thrombosis and Embolism
Occupation: 1900 in Palo Pinto County, Texas; Farmer
Occupation: 1910 in Strawn, Texas; Carpenter
Occupation: 1920 in Weatherford, Texas; Carpenter
Occupation: 1930 in Strawn, Texas; Painter
Occupation: 1940 in Strawn, Texas; Painter

Notes for Isaac Mansfield Edwards:
Death certificate gives date of birth as February 1, 1868. 1900 U.S. census gives date of birth
as February 1868. Headstone gives date of birth as February 1, 1870.

More About Mary Sophronia (Onie) Strawn:
Burial: 18 Feb 1950 in Mount Marion Cemetery, Strawn, Texas
Cause Of Death: Obstructive Jaundice

Notes for Mary Sophronia (Onie) Strawn:
Death certificate gives date of birth as April 11, 1874. 1900 U.S. census gives date of birth as
April 1874. Headstone gives date of birth as April 11, 1875.

Isaac Mansfield Edwards and Mary Sophronia (Onie) Strawn had the following children:

    i. MURRAY ARDIS[4] EDWARDS was born on 05 Jul 1900 in Strawn, Texas. He died on 16 Aug
1944 in Dallas, Texas. He married Johnie Belle Burt, daughter of John Frederick Burt
and Anna Belle Miller on 25 May 1922. She was born on 02 May 1898. She died on 20
Jan 1986 in Tarrant County, Texas.

More About Murray Ardis Edwards:
Burial: 16 Aug 1944 in Mount Marion Cemetery, Strawn, Texas
Cause Of Death: Brain Tumor - benign
Occupation: 1930; Bank Cashier, Loraine, Texas
Occupation: 1944; Collector for Internal Revenue Service

    ii.   ALLEN NEWTON EDWARDS was born on 24 Apr 1902 in Texas. He died in Feb 1979
in Tulsa, Oklahoma. He married ALLIE EDITH HERRIN. She was born on 13 Feb
1905. She died in Feb 1991.

    iii.   CHARLES EDWARDS.

26.   **AMBROSE EDWIN[3] EDWARDS** (Ambrose Newton[2], Ambrose[1]) was born on 20 Mar 1872 in Sulphur
Springs, Texas. He died on 15 Feb 1963 in Dallas, Texas. He married Anne Buntin Yarbrough,
daughter of George Yarbrough and Margaret Augusta Herrin on 03 Jul 1901 in Grayson County,
Texas. She was born on 15 Oct 1871 in Tyler, Texas. She died on 24 Oct 1955 in Dallas, Texas.

More About Ambrose Edwin Edwards:
Burial: 18 Feb 1963 in Restland Cemetery, Dallas, Texas
Cause Of Death: Cerebral Arteriosclerosis
Occupation: 1910 in Greenville, Texas; Real Estate Agent

Occupation: 1920 in Greenville, Texas; Real Estate Agent
Occupation: 1930 in Greenville, Texas; Farm Loan Agent
Occupation: 1940 in Dallas, Texas; Real Estate Proprietor

Notes for Ambrose Edwin Edwards:
Middle name of Edwin is probably after Doctor Edwin P. Becton of Sulphur Springs, Texas.

 Birth date is from Social Security death index. Headstone has 1871 for year of birth but this would conflict with the birth date of his brother, Walter White Edwards.

More About Anne Buntin Yarbrough:
Burial: 25 Oct 1955 in Restland Cemetery, Dallas, Texas
Cause Of Death: Coronary Occlusion

Ambrose Edwin Edwards and Anne Buntin Yarbrough had the following children:

     i.   AMBROSE YARBROUGH[4] EDWARDS was born on 16 Sep 1904 in Greeneville, Texas. He died on 18 Mar 1999 in Dallas, Texas. He married Mary Ruth Howell, daughter of Zebbie Lee Howell and Laura Annie Middleton on 09 Aug 1935 in Greenville, Texas. She was born on 06 Sep 1905 in Richland, Texas. She died on 31 Dec 1998.

         More About Ambrose Yarbrough Edwards:
         Burial: Restland Cemetery, Dallas, Texas
         Occupation: 1930 ; Accountant at automobile dealer, Greenville, Texas

     ii.   GEORGE NEWTON EDWARDS was born on 01 May 1908 in Texas. He died on 28 Apr 1955 in University Park, Dallas County, Texas. He married THERESA BRYAN. She was born on 10 Sep 1907. She died on 29 Jul 1992.

         More About George Newton Edwards:
         Burial: 29 Apr 1955 in Restland Cemetery, Dallas, Texas Cause Of Death: Malignant Brain Tumor
         Occupation: Sales Representative

27.   MCDONALD[3] EDWARDS (Ambrose Newton[2], Ambrose[1]) was born on 10 Dec 1877 in Strawn, Texas. He died on 08 Nov 1957 in Lubbock, Texas. He married Sally May Marchbanks, daughter of Finley W. Marchbanks and Sarah A. Hix on 26 Feb 1899 in Strawn, Texas. She was born on 12 Feb 1877 in Cleburne, Texas. She died on 27 Oct 1957 in Fort Worth, Texas.

More About McDonald Edwards:
Burial: 08 Nov 1957 in O'Donnell Cemetery, O'Donnell, Texas
Cause Of Death: Nephrosclerosis
Occupation: 1900 in Palo Pinto County, Texas; Hack Man
Occupation: 1910 in Palo Pinto County, Texas; Lumber Merchant
Occupation: 1920 in Palo Pinto County, Texas; Lumber Merchant
Occupation: 1930 in O'Donnell, Texas; Lumber Yard Manager
Occupation: 1940 in O'Donnell, Texas; Lumber Yard Proprietor

More About Sally May Marchbanks:
Burial: 28 Oct 1957 in O'Donnell Cemetery, O'Donnell, Texas
Cause Of Death: Chronic Myocarditis

Notes for Sally May Marchbanks:
Headstone gives name as Sallie May instead of Sally May.

McDonald Edwards and Sally May Marchbanks had the following children:

    i. MARION WIRT[4] EDWARDS was born on 24 Aug 1901 in Strawn, Texas. He died on 07 Sep 1971 in Arlington, Tarrant County, Texas. He married Mary Elizabeth Gray on 30 Apr 1938 in Arlington, Texas. She was born on 18 Sep 1910 in Dallas, Texas. She died in 1999.

    More About Marion Wirt Edwards:
    Burial: 09 Sep 1971 in Moore Memorial Gardens, Arlington,
    Texas Cause Of Death: ; Cerebral Thrombosis
    Occupation: City Secretary of Arlington, Texas
    Occupation: Bookkeper for Vandergriff Chevrolet in Arlington, Texas
    Occupation: Secretary - Treasurer for Midway Savings and Loan, Arlington, Texas

    ii. LOUISE EDWARDS was born about 1913 in Texas. She married WILBER LINE.

28.   LEROY ARDIS[3] EDWARDS (Ambrose Newton[2], Ambrose[1]) was born on 27 Feb 1881 in Sulphur Springs, Texas. He died on 05 Dec 1951 in Loraine, Texas. He married (1) **EMMA GEORGIE IRENE GARLAND**, daughter of Edward Warren Garland and Julia Rebecca Kimbell on 27 Jul 1921 in Roscoe, Texas. She was born on 23 Mar 1880 in Annona, Texas. She died on 17 Dec 1969 in Kerrville, Texas. He married (2) **ADA MAY LOFLIN**, daughter of Daniel Vance Loflin and Margarite Sophia Crawley on 21 Nov 1906 in Palo Pinto County, Texas. She was born on 26 Apr 1886 in Palo Pinto County, Texas. She died on 15 Apr 1918 in Loraine, Texas.

More About LeRoy Ardis Edwards:
Burial: 07 Dec 1951 in Loraine Cemetery, Loraine,
Texas Cause Of Death: Carcinoma of Lung
Occupation: 1910 in Brazoria County, Texas; Truck Farmer
Occupation: 1918 in Ranger, Eastland County, Texas; Manager of Buell Lumber Company
Occupation: 1920 in Loraine, Texas; Lumber Yard Manager
Occupation: 1930 in Loraine, Texas; Lumber Yard Manager
Occupation: 1940 in Olton, Texas; Retail Lumber Yard Manager
Occupation: 1942 in Olton, Lamb County, Texas; Manager of Higgingbotham Lumber

Company Notes for LeRoy Ardis Edwards:

    Discovered and operated, with his brother Walter, "Baking Powder" gold mine near Rosedale, New Mexico.

    Dear Mr. Edwards:
    Your request to our Geological Information Center for information on the Baking Powder mine was forwarded to me. Probably fewer than a half-dozen living people in all the southwest have even heard of
this property as it is one of the more obscure such in all New Mexico. I am not aware that the property was ever examined by a trained geologist or engineer (unless your Edwards relatives were such and there is no known surviving record of their work). My extensive mines and prospects files are absolutely silent in regard to the Baking Powder. Nevertheless I have noted one or two very obscure references in my research.

The Baking Powder is located in the Rosedale Mining District at the extreme north end of the San Mateo mountains in southern Socorro county, New Mexico. I have not examined the mining claim records in the local courthouse for exact dates (mainly because you are the very first individual to ever request information on the property!) but would predict the claim (or claims) was located during latter part of the 19th century -- poss. mid-1890s -- as a result of the success of the well-known Rosedale mine and discovery of the nearby White Cap.

The "veins" in the Rosedale district are actually brecciated shear zones in the volcanic (rhyolitic) rocks The brecciated and sheared rhyolite has been recemented with a hard, bluish-white quartz and later with a clearer vein-type quartz. The entire vein mass is highly silicified and in those areas yielding the best gold values are heavily stained with the black and red oxides of manganese and iron respectively. Gold occurred in the native state in the upper oxidized portions of the vein but is very nearly absent in the sulfide portion at or below the water table. Remarkably, little or no silver is present. I would predict the Baking Powder "vein" to be similar in character to the above. Dr. Charles Ferguson's doctoral dissertation covered a large area extending from the southern end of the Rosedale District to the north well beyond White Cap and Big Rosa canyons. I asked Charlie if he knew the locality of the Baking Powder and other prospects and he indicated approximate locations for two unnamed mine workings about two miles north and northwest of the Rosedale which I feel are the White Cap and the Baking Powder. The projected location for the latter is approx. Sec3, T6S, R6W near the head of Big Rosa canyon.

Soon after the turn of the century, development on the Baking Powder had apparently progressed to the mining stage. According to a note in the Engineering and Mining Journal, 24 December 1903, p 988, the Baking Powder mine was said to be initiating "full operations," whatever that meant; Walter Edwards, undoubtedly your ancestor, was the manager. Unfortunately the operation failed to live up to expectations and within four years was facing foreclosure for $1200 in back wages (Soccoro Chieftan, 30 November 1907). The obvious conclusion is that the mine failed to develop pay ore in sufficient quantities to sustain the operation and it failed. And that is the current extent of the "historic" record!

I and my colleagues attempted to visit this prospect in May 2000, but despite our "approximate" location on the topo sheet, and a full day's search, four-wheeling, etc., we failed to locate it. I should note that the 'road' up Big Rosa canyon is, in places, a figment of the imagination -- we could have easily missed a small prospect off in the ponderosas! The Mount Whithington jeep road may pass within a mile of the mine on the west and that is the route I will next attempt.

Now that you have made a request for information, I shall keep a sharp lookout for additional data. I must yet peruse the pages of the few issues of the San Marcial Bee that have survived the ravages of time and will keep you in mind should anything materialize. Additionally I will examine the claim location records upon my next visit to the courthouse. On the other hand, I'd be most pleased to add to our archival files any information you'd be willing to share with us from your family's papers. Regards,

Robert W. Eveleth Senior
Mining Engineer Curator,
Mining Archives

Dear Mr. Edwards:

Recent research on several articles of local mining interest has, once again, led me through the pages of the Socorro Chieftain. Recalling your interest in the above, I made a copy of an article on the Baking Powder/Edwards Bros., reproduced below in its entirety:

Socorro Chieftain, 6/14/1902, p 4: "Rosedale, N. M., June 10m, 1902 -- Editor Chieftain -- Rosedale is quiet at present. Big Rosa, 2-1/2 miles to the northwest, shows great and rapidly increasing activity. Fully $5,000 worth of work is now underway and other contracts are being let. The immediate cause of this work was the discovery and partial development of the Baking Powder property of the Edwards Brothers of El Paso, Tex. This claim showed well from the surface but now at a depth of 55 feet it is exciting old time prospectors and tenderfeet alike by yielding a strong vein of high grade ore while picked samples show as high as 84 ounces in gold. Two or more stamp mills, stores, drink emporiums, a post office, dozens of cabins and tents, a good graded road up

Big Rosa, and a couple of hundred men tearing into its mountain sides may be a vision, but as a miner and prospector of long experience I think this and more will be a reality within 12 months. Big Rosa may not be as good a mining camp as Cripple Creek, Colo. It may be better. The writer has no interest there and is not puffing the camp to "induce capital," but is sincere in saying that right now is a suitable and very favorable time to investigate Big Rosa.

There can be no harm in keeping an eye on the indicator." Signed: A. L. Heister."

As I continue to go through the pages of the Socorro Chieftan, I'll be sure to let you know if the writer's dream materialized.

Best Regards,
Robert W. Eveleth
Senior Mining Engineer

More About Emma Georgie Irene Garland:
Burial: 20 Dec 1969 in Loraine Cemetery, Loraine, Texas
Cause Of Death: Broncho Pneumonia and Arteriosclerosis

More About LeRoy Ardis Edwards and Emma Georgie Irene Garland:
Marriage License: 27 Jul 1921 in Mitchell County, Texas
Marriage Fact: Married by S. H. Young, M.G.

LeRoy Ardis Edwards and Emma Georgie Irene Garland had the following child:

i. ROY GARLAND[4] EDWARDS was born on 30 May 1922 in Loraine, Texas. He died on 14 Oct 1974 in Tampa, Florida. He married Maribel Savage, daughter of William Payne Savage and Mary Bell Badgett on 08 Apr 1944 in Lubbock, Texas. She was born on 22 Jun 1926 in Sherman, Texas. She died on 14 Feb 2010 in Tampa, Florida.

More About Roy Garland Edwards:
Burial: 17 Oct 1974 in Pleasant Grove Cemetery, Durant, Florida
Cause Of Death: Heart Failure
Occupation: 1940 in Olton, Texas; Repairman
Military Service: Bet. 1942-1964; U.S. Air Force (Major)

Notes for Roy Garland Edwards:
Died at the base hospital on MacDill Air Force Base.

More About Ada May Loflin:
Burial: Mount Marion Cemetery, Strawn, Texas

LeRoy Ardis Edwards and Ada May Loflin had the following children:

ii. ESTHA LOUISE EDWARDS was born on 07 Apr 1908 in Ranger, Texas. She died on 23 May 1994 in Abilene, Texas. She married Floyd Franklin Coffee, son of Thomas Joshua Coffee and Hannah Pauline Dorn on 24 Aug 1934 in Snyder, Texas. He was born on 01 Dec 1900 in Mitchell County, Texas. He died on 19 Feb 1994 in Loraine, Texas.

More About Estha Louise Edwards:
Burial: Loraine, Texas

Occupation: 1930 in Loraine, Mitchell County, Texas; Public School Teacher

Notes for Estha Louise Edwards:
Head stone gives April 7, 1908 as birth date. Social Security Death Index gives April17, 1908 as birth date.

    iii.   MARVIN YOUNG EDWARDS was born on 20 Sep 1910 in Alvin, Texas. He died on 19 Jan 1985 in Abilene, Texas. He married (1) EVELYN VIRGINIA COX, daughter of Bluford Sanford Cox and Mary Maud Baze on 15 Jun 1935 in Mitchell County, Texas. She was born on 11 May 1913 in Bay City, Texas. She died on 16 Feb 1979 in Abilene, Taylor County, Texas. He married (2) LAURA ALICE FERGUSON, daughter of Charles C. Ferguson and Annie Ruth Martin on 24 Sep 1981 in Jones County, Texas. She was born on 21 Sep 1919 in McCaulley, Fisher County, Texas. She died on 26 Jul 1994 in Abilene, Texas.

More About Marvin Young Edwards:
Burial: Elmwood Memorial Park, Abilene, Texas
Living In: 1940 Sweetwater, Texas
Occupation: 1930 in Loraine, Mitchell County, Texas; Lumber Yard Book Keeper
Occupation: 1940 in Sweetwater, Nolan County, Texas; Office Clerk in Morrison Supply Company
Military Service: Bet. 05 Nov 1943-03 Jan 1946 ; U. S. Navy

    iv.   MARGARET RUTH EDWARDS was born on 18 Jan 1917 in Loraine, Texas. She died on 26 Dec 1984 in Tempe, Arizona. She married William Glenn Johnson, son of Edgar Francis Johnson and Ada Eva Jennings on 25 Sep 1939 in Phoenix, Arizona. He was born on 12 Aug 1910 in Statesville, Tennessee. He died on 28 Jan 1988 in Tempe, Arizona.

29.   BECTON GOODSON[3] EDWARDS (Ambrose Newton[2], Ambrose[1]) was born on 29 Oct 1884 in Sulphur Springs, Texas. He died on 04 Dec 1960 in Dallas, Dallas County, Texas. He married Minnie Mae Strain, daughter of George Douglas Strain and Sarah Elizabeth Strawn on 04 Nov 1908 in Weatherford, Texas. She was born on 22 Feb 1887 in Strawn, Texas. She died on 28 Jul 1956 in Corsicana, Navarro County, Texas.

More About Becton Goodson Edwards:
Burial: 06 Dec 1960 in Grove Hill Cemetery, Dallas, Dallas County, Texas
Cause Of Death: Coronary Occlusion, Arteriosclerosis Heart Valve
Occupation: 1910 in Weatherford, Texas; Real Estate and Insurance Salesman
Occupation: 1920 in Forney, Texas; Postmaster
Occupation: 1930 in Forney, Texas; Pharmacist
Occupation: 1940 in Forney, Texas; Retail Drug Store Manager

Notes for Becton Goodson Edwards:
Named after Doctor Edwin P. Becton of Sulphur Springs, Texas. Doctor Becton served in the 22nd Texas Infantry, C.S.A., during the Civil War and is buried in Sulphur Springs City Cemetery, Sulphur Springs, Texas.

More About Minnie Mae Strain:
Burial: 28 Jul 1956 in Grove Hill Cemetery, Dallas, Dallas County, Texas
Cause Of Death: Cerebral Hemorrhage

Notes for Minnie Mae Strain:
Death certificate has her middle name spelled "May". Headstone has her middle name
spelled "Mae".

More About Becton Goodson Edwards and Minnie Mae Strain:
Marriage License: 03 Nov 1908 in Parker County, Texas
Marriage Fact: Married by George M. Oakley, Minister of the Gospel

Becton Goodson Edwards and Minnie Mae Strain had the following children:

    i. LOIS ELIZABETH[4] EDWARDS was born on 16 Sep 1909 in Texas. She died on 08 Jul 1993
in Bexar County, Texas. She married (UNKNOWN) WADE.

        More About Lois Elizabeth Edwards:
        Living In: 1993 San Antonio, Bexar County, Texas
        Occupation: 1930 in Forney, Texas; Public SchoolTeacher

    ii.   ERNEST WELDON EDWARDS was born on 03 Dec 1910 in Texas. He died on 15
Mar 1945 in Island of Iwo Jima. He married MARIE GARRETT. She was born on 08
Feb 1908 in Texas. She died on 18 Nov 1950 in Dallas, Dallas County, Texas.

        More About Ernest Weldon Edwards:
        Burial: 21 Mar 1949 in National Memorial Cemetery of the
        Pacific.
        Living In: 1935 Dallas, Dallas County, Texas
        Occupation: 1930 in Forney, Texas; Garage Mechanic
        Occupation: 1940 in Dallas, Dallas County, Texas; Sandwich Shop
        Manager
        Military Service: United States Marine Corps, World War Two

        Notes for Ernest Weldon Edwards:
        Died during the assault of Iwo Jima in World war Two.

        Graduate of SMU.

    iii.   RUTH EDWARDS was born on 10 Aug 1912 in Tyler, Texas. She died on 05 Sep
2004 in Dallas, Texas. She married Albert Lee Greer in 1938. He was born on
04 Apr 1911 in Dallas, Texas. He died on 09 Nov 2001 in Dallas, Texas.

        More About Ruth Edwards:
        Burial: 09 Sep 2004 in Grove Hill Memorial Park, Dallas, Texas

        Notes for Ruth Edwards:
        GREER, RUTH EDWARDS, was born August 10, 1912 in Tyler, Texas to Becton G.
        and Minnie Mae Edwards. She passed away September 5, 2004 in Dallas, Texas.
        Ruth grew up in Forney, Texas, moving to Dallas in the early 30's. She was President
        of the PTA at Lakewood Elementary, J.L. Long Middle School, Woodrow Wilson High
        School, a longtime member of the East Dallas Ladies Kiwanis Club and a member of
        Highland Park United Methodist Church since 1940. For her entire adult life she was
        the glue that held a large extended family together. She was preceded in death by her
        husband, A.L. Greer. Survived by her daughter, Anne Greer Lasky of Dallas; son,
        Thomas Andrew Greer and his partner, Brian Falk of

Taos, N.M.; sister, Margaret Robinson of Beaumont, Texas. Open visitation Tuesday, 12:00 - 9:00 P.M. at Sparkman/Hillcrest Funeral Home. Funeral services 2:00 P.M. Wednesday at Sparkman/Hillcrest Northwest Hwy. Chapel, Rev. Bill Smith, officiating. Interment to follow at Grove Hill Memorial Park. If desired, memorials may be made to the Lighthouse for the Blind, 4245 Office Parkway, Dallas, Texas 75204. Dignity Memorial Sparkman Hillcrest 7405 W. Northwest Hwy. Dallas (214) 363-5401

Published in Dallas Morning News from Sept. 6 to Sept. 7, 2004

iv.　GEORGE ARDIS EDWARDS was born on 16 Jul 1914 in Forney, Texas. He died on 13 Nov 1953 in Austin, Travis County, Texas.

More About George Ardis Edwards:
Burial: Grove Hill Memorial Park, Dallas, Dallas County, Texas
Cause Of Death: Coronary Occlusions
Living In: 1953　Dallas, Dallas County, Texas
Occupation: Accountant Clerk with Power and Light Company
Military Service: U.S. Navy - World War Two

v.　MARVIN BECTON EDWARDS was born on 22 Nov 1923 in Texas. He died on 01 Feb 1973. He married Patricia Ann White on 25 Jun 1946 in Terrell County, Texas. She was born on 03 Mar 1928 in Terrell County, Texas. She died in Jan 2003 in Longview, Texas.

More About Marvin Becton Edwards:
Living In: 1961 Longview, Texas
Military Service: 04 Nov 1942 in Dallas, Dallas County, Texas; Enlisted in U.S. Army Air Force

Notes for Marvin Becton Edwards:
Served as navigator on a B-17. Was shot down near Dusseldorf, Germany and held as Prisoner of War for a year and a half.
----

vi.　MARGARET ANNE EDWARDS was born on 04 Sep 1929 in Forney, Kaufman County, Texas. She died on 17 Jun 2011 in Silsbee, Texas. She married (1) JOHN PATRICK MOONEYHAM, son of Jesse Mooneyham and Hazel N. Easterly on 24 Sep 1947. He was born on 17 Mar 1929 in Kemp, Texas. He died on 23 Oct 2000 in Silsbee, Texas. She married (2) ROBERT RAY ROBINSON on 28 Feb 1981 in Jefferson County, Texas. He was born on 10 Jun 1944. He died on 28 Sep 2005 in Beaumont, Texas.

More About Margaret Anne Edwards:
Burial: 21 Jun 2011 in Forest Lawn Memorial Park Cemetery and Funeral Home, Beaumont, Texas

30.　**TULLY DECATUR LAMAR**[3] **EDWARDS** (Charles Anderson Brown[2], Ambrose[1]) was born on 28 Dec 1870 in Dale County, Alabama. He died on 06 Feb 1942 in Dothan, Houston County, Alabama. He married Claudia Blackman on 22 Feb 1894 in Ozark, Alabama. She was born in Jan 1873 in

Alabama. She died on 23 Nov 1954 in Coffee County, Alabama.

More About Tully Decatur Lamar Edwards:
Burial: 08 Feb 1942 in Union Cemetery, Ozark, Alabama
Occupation: 1901 in Enterprise, Alabama; Notary Public, Appointed August 26, 1901
and commissioned September 5, 1901.
Occupation: 1904 in Enterprise, Alabama; Notary Public. Appointed September 30, 1904
and commissioned October 19, 1904
Occupation: 1910 in Enterprise, Alabama; Farm Overseer
Occupation: 1920 in Enterprise, Alabama; Works with
Livestock
Occupation: 1930 in Enterprise, Alabama; Salesman
Occupation: 1940 in Enterprise, Alabama; Travelling Salesman for Shoe Factory

More About Claudia Blackman:
Burial: Union Cemetery, Ozark, Alabama
Occupation: 1930 in Enterprise, Alabama; Music Teacher
Occupation: 1940 in Enterprise, Alabama; Music Teacher

More About Tully Decatur Lamar Edwards and Claudia Blackman:
Marriage Fact: Married by P. L. Mosely, MG

Tully Decatur Lamar Edwards and Claudia Blackman had the following children:

    i.   HARISON B.[4] EDWARDS was born on 28 Feb 1895. He died on 17 Jun 1895.

        More About Harison B. Edwards:
        Burial: Union Cemetery, Ozark, Dale County, Alabama

    ii.   KENNETH B. EDWARDS was born in Nov 1896 in Alabama.

        More About Kenneth B. Edwards:
        Living In: 1920 Living With His Parents in Enterprise, Alabama
        Occupation: 1920 in Enterprise, Alabama; Teacher

    iii.   FRANKLIN LAMAR EDWARDS was born on 17 Jul 1899 in Alabama. He died on 11 Aug 1966 in Dothan, Houston County, Alabama.

        More About Franklin Lamar Edwards:
        Burial: Union Cemetery, Ozark, Alabama
        Living In: 1930 Living With His Parents in Enterprise, Alabama
        Living In: 1940 Living With His Parents in Enterprise, Alabama
        Occupation: 1930 in Enterprise, Alabama; Salesman
        Occupation: 1940 in Enterprise, Alabama; Janitor in County Court House

    iv.   (INFANT SON) EDWARDS was born on 13 Sep 1902. He died on 13 Sep 1902.

31.   EURA EMELINE AMANDA[3] EDWARDS (Charles Anderson Brown[2], Ambrose[1]) was born on 28 Nov 1871 in Dale County, Alabama. She died on 16 Apr 1960 in Ozark, Alabama. She married Joseph Harris Adams, son of Joseph A. Adams and Annie Laurie Kirksey on 11 Oct 1891 in Ozark, Alabama. He was born on 12 Aug 1870 in Newton, Dale County, Alabama. He died on 13 Jan 1918 in Houston County, Alabama.

More About Eura Emeline Amanda
Edwards: Burial: Union Cemetery, Ozark,
Alabama
Living In: 1920 Ozark, Alabama
Living In: 1930 Ozark, Alabama
Living In: 1940 Living with her son, Samuel Kirke Adams, and his family in Ozark, Alabama

More About Joseph Harris Adams:
Burial: Union Cemetery, Ozark, Alabama
Occupation: 1900 in Ozark, Alabama; Newspaper Publisher
Occupation: 1910 in Ozark, Alabama; Newspaper Publisher

More About Joseph Harris Adams and Eura Emeline Amanda Edwards:
Marriage Fact: Married by A. L. Sellers, MG

Joseph Harris Adams and Eura Emeline Amanda Edwards had the following children:

    i.   JOSEPH HARRIS[4] ADAMS was born on 08 Jul 1892 in Dale County, Alabama. He died on 14 Oct 1897 in Dale County, Alabama.

        Notes for Joseph Harris Adams: Died in infancy.

    ii.   BESS HENDERSON ADAMS was born on 10 Dec 1893 in Dale County, Alabama. She died on 03 Jun 1985 in Ozark, Alabama.

        Notes for Bess Henderson Adams: Never married.

    iii.   CHARLES HARRIS ADAMS was born on 10 Feb 1899 in Ozark, Alabama. He died on 30 Apr 1968 in Dothan. Alabama. He married Willela Milligan on 14 Dec 1925. She was born on 13 Dec 1905 in Newton, Alabama. She died on 09 Jun 1984 in Dothan, Alabama.

    iv.   SAMUEL KIRKE ADAMS was born on 08 Jan 1901 in Ozark, Alabama. He died on 17 Apr 1991 in Ozark, Alabama. He married Eleanor Wallace, daughter of G. O. Wallace and Mary McEachern on 21 Jul 1935 in Dale County, Alabama. She was born on 27 May 1906. She died on 18 Feb 1989.

        More About Samuel Kirke Adams:
        Burial: Ozark, Alabama
        Occupation: 1930 in Ozark, Alabama; Salesman
        Occupation: 1940 in Ozark, Alabama; Fertilizer Salesman
        Occupation: Bet. 1940-1944 ; Mayor of Ozark, Alabama

    v.   WILLIAM ROGER ADAMS was born on 15 Jun 1904 in Dale County, Alabama. He died on 19 Apr 1967 in Charlotte, North Carolina. He married Lois Sidney Jones on 10 Aug 1927 in Ozark, Alabama. She was born on 02 Jan 1907.

    vi.   ANNIE MARTHA ADAMS was born on 21 Jul 1906 in Dale County, Alabama. She died on 15 Dec 1958 in Ozark, Alabama. She married Louie Tamplin on 16 Jun 1934 in Ozark, Alabama. He was born on 03 Aug 1905 in Auburn, Alabama. He died on 25 Sep 1981 in Ozark, Alabama.

More About Annie Martha Adams:
Burial: Westview Cemetery, Ozark, Alabama
Occupation: 1930 in Ozark, Alabama; Public School Teacher

32.   LILLIAN VIRGINIA[3] EDWARDS (Charles Anderson Brown[2], Ambrose[1]) was born on 29 Jul 1876 in Dale County, Alabama. She died on 22 Jan 1914 in Enterprise, Alabama. She married Jackson Maryland Young, son of William Young and Mary Davenport on 24 Mar 1901 in Ozark, Alabama. He was born on 07 Jan 1873 in Pine Level, Alabama. He died on 11 Nov 1949 in St. Petersburg, Florida.

More About Lillian Virginia Edwards:
Burial: 24 Jan 1914 in Enterprise City Cemetery, Enterprise, Alabama

Notes for Lillian Virginia Edwards:
1900 U. S. census has her birth as July 1875. Headstone has July 29, 1876.

More About Jackson Maryland Young:
Burial: 14 Nov 1949 in Enterprise City Cemetery, Enterprise, Alabama
Living In: 1935 St. Petersburg, Florida
Occupation: 1910 in Hattiesburg, Mississippi; College English Teacher
Occupation: 1917 in Enterprise, Alabama; Farmer
Occupation: 1920 in Birmingham, Alabama; Steel Mill Foreman
Occupation: 1930 in Birmingham, Alabama; Real Estate Owner
Occupation: 1940 in St. Petersburg, Florida; Retired

Jackson Maryland Young and Lillian Virginia Edwards had the following children:

   i.   MARYLAND VIRGINIA[4] YOUNG was born on 18 Oct 1902 in Houston, Mississippi. She married FRANK L. MCEWEN. He was born about 1897 in Mississippi.

   ii. JACKSON MARYLAND YOUNG was born on 31 Dec 1906 in Wesson, Mississippi. He died on 08 Feb 1968 in Niagra Falls, New York.

        More About Jackson Maryland Young:
        Occupation: 1930 in Birmingham, Alabama; Office Clerk in Steel Mill

   iii. EMILY CAROLYN YOUNG was born on 26 Dec 1908 in Hattiesburg, Mississippi. She married Owen Willard Chase on 19 Jan 1953 in Adele, Georgia. He was born on 18 Apr 1907. He died on 25 May 1960.

        More About Emily Carolyn Young:
        Living In: 1940 Living with her father in St. Petersburg, Florida.
        Occupation: 1940 in St. Petersburg, Florida; Filing Clerk

   iv. CHARLES FIELDING YOUNG was born on 14 Oct 1912 in Enterprise, Alabama. He died on 14 Oct 1969.

        More About Charles Fielding Young:
        Living In: 1920 Living with his aunt, Rena Carolyn Edwards, and her family in Ozark, Alabama

Living In: 1930 Living with his aunt, Rena Carolyn Edwards, and her family in Ozark, Alabama

33. **RENA CAROLYN**[3] **EDWARDS** (Charles Anderson Brown[2], Ambrose[1]) was born on 21 Jul 1878 in Dale County, Alabama. She died on 22 Oct 1978 in Talledega, Alabama. She married Clifford Malone Cox, son of Willis S. Cox and Hattie Wingate on 28 Apr 1900 in Ozark, Alabama. He was born on 17 Apr 1871 in Alabama. He died on 03 Feb 1932 in Dothan, Houston County, Alabama.

More About Rena Carolyn Edwards:
Burial: Union Cemetery, Ozark, Alabama
Occupation: 1940 in Ozark, Alabama; Book Work for W.P.A.

More About Clifford Malone Cox:
Burial: Union Cemetery, Ozark,
Alabama
Occupation: 1900 in Ozark, Alabama; Town Marshall
Occupation: 1910 in Ozark, Alabama; Post Master
Occupation: 1920 in Ozark, Alabama; Can not read occupation on U.S. 1920
census
Occupation: 1930 in Ozark, Alabama; Post Master

More About Clifford Malone Cox and Rena Carolyn Edwards:
Marriage Fact: Married by G. N. Winslett

Clifford Malone Cox and Rena Carolyn Edwards had the following child:

      i. HEZZ MALONE[4] COX was born on 31 May 1903 in Ozark, Alabama. He died on 01 Oct 1965 in Talladega, Alabama.

34. **HIRAM FLOURNOY**[3] **EDWARDS** (Charles Anderson Brown[2], Ambrose[1]) was born on 14 Dec 1883 in Dale County, Alabama. He died on 25 Feb 1971 in Ozark, Dale County, Alabama. He married Lena Rebecca Johnson, daughter of Henry Johnson and Evie Sellers on 09 Jun 1912 in Enterprise, Alabama. She was born on 28 Sep 1894 in Ozark, Alabama. She died on 11 Nov 1971 in Ozark, Dale County, Alabama.

More About Hiram Flournoy Edwards:
Burial: 27 Feb 1971 in Morning View Cemetery, Ozark, Alabama
Living In: 1910 Living with his parents in Ozark, Alabama
Occupation: 1910 in Ozark, Alabama; Rural Route Mail Carrier
Occupation: 1920 in Ozark, Alabama; Rural Route Mail Carrier
Occupation: 1930 in Ozark, Alabama; Government Worker
Occupation: 1940 in Ozark, Alabama; No Occupation Listed on U.S. 1940 U.S. census

Notes for Hiram Flournoy Edwards:
Identical twin of Walter Leroy Edwards.
World War One draft registration has his name as Hiram Flurnoy Edwards. His signature on the card verifies this.

More About Lena Rebecca Johnson:
Burial: 13 Nov 1971 in Morning View Cemetery, Ozark, Alabama

Hiram Flournoy Edwards and Lena Rebecca Johnson had the following children:

      i.   MARTHA EVELYN[4] EDWARDS was born on 03 May 1913 in Ozark, Alabama.

      ii.   HIRAM FLOURNOY EDWARDS was born on 23 Dec 1915 in Ozark, Alabama. He died on 15 May 1982 in Ozark, Alabama. He married Eloise Southard in 1941 in Walton County, Florida.

More About Hiram Flournoy Edwards:
Burial: Morning View Cemetery, Ozark, Alabama
Living In: 1940 Living with his parents in Ozark, Alabama
Occupation: 1940 in Ozark, Alabama; Travelling Salesman for Snuff Company
Military Service: Bet. 17 Oct 1942-25 Nov 1945; U.S. Army, World War Two (MSgt)

Notes for Hiram Flournoy Edwards:
Enlisted in U.S. Army October 17, 1942 at Fort McClellan, Alabama.

Marriage record spells his middle name "Flournoy".
----

   iii.   LENA FRANCES EDWARDS was born on 16 Jul 1918 in Ozark, Alabama.

   iv.   EURA CAROLYN EDWARDS was born on 18 Feb 1921 in Ozark, Alabama.

More About Eura Carolyn Edwards: Occupation:
1940 in Ozark, Alabama; Saleslady

   v.   ANNE ELIZABETH EDWARDS was born on 19 Jan 1924 in Ozark, Alabama. She died on 14 Apr 1988.

35.   WALTER LEROY[3] EDWARDS (Charles Anderson Brown[2], Ambrose[1]) was born on 14 Dec 1883 in Dale County, Alabama. He died on 08 Dec 1975 in Ozark, Alabama. He married Mary Tom Ray on 21 May 1912 in Ozark, Alabama. She was born on 31 Aug 1892 in Brundidge, Alabama. She died on 04 Nov 1967 in Ozark, Alabama.

More About Walter Leroy Edwards:
Burial: Westview Cemetery, Ozark, Dale County, Alabama
Living In: 1910 Living with his parents in Ozark, Alabama
Occupation: 1910 in Ozark, Alabama; Clerk for Oil Company
Occupation: 1918 in Ozark, Alabama; Book Keeper in Mutual Cotton Oil Company
Occupation: 1920 in Ozark, Alabama; Oil Mill Manager
Occupation: 1930 in Ozark, Alabama; Superintendent at Mill
Occupation: 1940 in Ozark, Alabama; Book Keeper at Olil Mill

Notes for Walter Leroy Edwards:
Identical Twin of Hiram Flournoy Edwards.
Social Security death index gives 1975 as year of death.

More About Mary Tom Ray:
Burial: Westview Cemetery, Ozark, Dale County, Alabama

Walter Leroy Edwards and Mary Tom Ray had the following children:
   i.   WALTER RAY[4] EDWARDS was born on 20 Sep 1917 in Ozark, Alabama. He died on 17 Jun 1978 in Troy, Alabama. He married Dorothy Ann Fuqua, daughter of James Fuqua and Hassie Roberts on 25 Dec 1936 in Elba, Alabama. She was born on 06 Dec 1919 in Loisville, Alabama. She died on 05 Jun 1979 in Troy, Alabama.

More About Walter Ray Edwards:
Burial: Westview Cemetery, Dale County, Alabama
Living In: 1940 Walter and his family are living with his parents in Ozark, Alabama.
Occupation: 1940 in Ozark, Alabama; Laborer at Filling Station

ii.   THOMAS LEROY EDWARDS was born on 03 Nov 1927 in Ozark, Alabama. He died on 03 Nov 1927 in Ozark, Alabama.

More About Thomas Leroy Edwards:
Burial: Union Cemetery, Ozark, Dale County, Alabama

36.   LUCILLE[3] EDWARDS (Charles Anderson Brown[2], Ambrose[1]) was born on 02 Jan 1890 in Dale County, Alabama. She died on 20 May 1969 in Geneva, Alabama. She married Frederick Malcolm Fleming, son of William Leroy Fleming and Mary Love Edwards on 24 Mar 1910 in Ozark, Alabama. He was born on 20 Jan 1888 in Brundidge, Alabama. He died on 09 Jan 1953 in Montgomery, Montgomery County, Alabama.

More About Lucille Edwards:
Burial: Geneva City Cemetery, Geneva, Alabama

More About Frederick Malcolm Fleming:

b: 20 Jan 1888 in Brundidge, Alabama
Burial: Geneva City Cemetery, Geneva, Alabama
Occupation: 1910 in Enterprise, Alabama; City School Teacher
Occupation: 1917 in Geneva County, Alabama; Livestock Dealer
Occupation: 1920 in Geneva, Geneva County, Alabama; Livestock Dealer
Occupation: 1930 in Geneva, Geneva County, Alabama; Building Contractor
Military Service: 1925 in Geneva County, Alabama; Captain in Battery E, 141st Field Artillery, Alabama National Guard

Frederick Malcolm Fleming and Lucille Edwards had the following children:
i.   MARTHA LOVE FLEMING was born on 14 Jul 1912. She died on 17 Jul 1912.

More About Martha Love Fleming:
Burial: Enterprise City Cemetery, Enterprise, Alabama

ii.   MARY CAROLINE FLEMING was born in Dec 1914 in Geneva, Geneva County, Alabama. She married AUBREY SKIPPER. He was born on 21 Oct 1912. He died in Jul 1973.

More About Mary Caroline Fleming: b: Dec 1914

iii.   FREDERICK MALCOLM FLEMING was born on 25 Apr 1921 in Geneva, Geneva County, Alabama. He died on 15 Sep 2000 in Geneva, Alabama. He married ANNA MARIE BALTZ. She was born on 15 Nov 1921. She died on 31 Mar 2000 in Joppa, alabama.

iv.   CHARLES WILLIAM FLEMING was born on 25 Nov 1925 in Geneva, Geneva County,

Alabama. He died on 28 May 1984 in Geneva, Geneva County, Alabama. He married Karol Ruth Latimer in 1952. She was born on 18 Aug 1931. She died in May 1983 in Geneva, Alabama.

More About Charles William Fleming:
b: 25 Nov 1925

37.   **WALTER A.**[3] **EDWARDS** (Walter Starr[2], Ambrose[1]) was born on 06 Nov 1871 in Coffee County, Alabama. He died on 14 May 1906 in Enterprise, Alabama. He married Rattie Clifford Warren, daughter of William Warren and Emeline Leslie Thompson about 1896. She was born in Apr 1872 in Alabama.

More About Walter A. Edwards:
Burial: Enterprise City Cemetery, Enterprise, Alabama
Occupation: 1900 in Enterprise, Alabama; General Merchandise Merchant

More About Rattie Clifford Warren:
Living In: 1910 Florala, Covington County, Alabama with her children as a widow.

Walter A. Edwards and Rattie Clifford Warren had the following children:

     i.   LEO GLENN[4] EDWARDS was born in Sep 1897 in Alabama. He married BILLIE (UNKNOWN). He married RUTH (UNKNOWN).

    ii.   EVELYN D. EDWARDS was born in Jan 1900 in Alabama. She married (UNKNOWN) HALL.

    iii.   OPHELIA PHEOBE EDWARDS was born about 1903 in Alabama. She married GRANT SWISHER.

38.   **LUDIE**[3] **EDWARDS** (Walter Starr[2], Ambrose[1]) was born about 1876 in Alabama. She died on 02 Jul 1931 in Montgomery, Alabama. She married Frank Glenn Park, son of Frank Park and Anne (unknown) on 08 Dec 1898 in Enterprise, Alabama. He was born in Apr 1859 in Alabama. He died on 26 May 1909 in Enterprise, Alabama.

More About Ludie Edwards:
Burial: Enterprise, Alabama
Living In: 1931 Enterprise. Alabama

Notes for Ludie Edwards:

1910 U.S. census indicates Ludie had three children with one still living in 1910.

Frank Glenn Park and Ludie Edwards had the following children:

    i.   ROBERT G.[4] PARK was born in Oct 1899 in Alabama. He died on 13 Oct 1904 in Pike County, Alabama.

           More About Robert G. Park:
           Burial: Hopewell Cemetery, Pike County, Alabama

    ii.   LUDIE ANNE PARK was born before Apr 1910 in Alabama.

39.   **HELENA AUGUSTA**[3] **EDWARDS** (Walter Starr[2], Ambrose[1]) was born on 31 Aug 1878 in Alabama.
She died on 24 Feb 1920 in Garrison, Geneva County, Alabama. She married Frank W. Enzor
on 21 Nov 1897 in Coffee County, Alabama. He was born on 03 Jul 1877 in Alabama. He died on
26 Jan 1968 in Crestview, Florida.

More About Helena Augusta Edwards:
Burial: Enterprise City Cemetery, Enterprise, Alabama

More About Frank W. Enzor:
Burial: Liveoak Park Memorial Cemetery, Crestview, Florida
Occupation: 1900 in Enterprise, Alabama; Merchant of General Merchandize
Occupation: 1910 in Hartford, Geneva County, Alabama; Laborer
Occupation: 1920 in Marl, Geneva County, Alabama; Turpentine Still Operator
Occupation: 1930 in Florala, Covington County, Florida; Picture Show Proprietor
Occupation: 1940 in Laurel hill, Okaloosa County, Florida; Foreman on W.P. A. Project

Notes for Frank W. Enzor:
World War One draft registration has Frank W. Enzor for name.

More About Frank W. Enzor and Helena Augusta
Edwards: Marriage Fact: Married by J.K. Powell, Minister

Frank W. Enzor and Helena Augusta Edwards had the following children:

i.   **SARAH FRANCES**[4] **ENZOR** was born on 10 Feb 1898 in Enterprise, Alabama. She
died on 07 Sep 1943. She married Zollie Avery Dozier, son of Green Berry
Dozier and Rebecca Arena Rowell on 05 Dec 1915 in Enterprise, Alabama. He
was born on 10 Oct 1885 in Dozier, Alabama. He died on 18 May 1965 in
Houston, Harris County, Texas.

More About Sarah Frances Enzor:
Occupation: 1930 in Houston, Texas; Lunch Room Waitress
Occupation: 1940 in Houston, Texas; School Cafeteria Operator

ii.   **LUDIE GLENN ENZOR** was born on 15 Mar 1902 in Alabama. She died on 16 Oct 1996 in
Walton County, Florida. She married **LANCELOT H. HUGHES**. He was born on
27 Dec 1893 in Ponce De Leon, Florida. He died on 14 Feb 1994 in
Destin, Okaloosa County, Florida.

iii.   **HELEN AUGUSTA ENZOR** was born on 12 Apr 1908 in Alabama. She died on 04 Nov
1987 in Okaloosa County, Florida. She married **VAN NESS BUTLER**. He was born on
21 Sep 1903 in Mine County, South Dakota. He died on 25 Aug 2000 in Santa
Rosa Beach, Florida.

More About Helen Augusta Enzor:
Burial: Magnolia Cemetery, DeFuniak Springs, Florida

iv.   **BESSIE M. ENZOR** was born on 26 Aug 1912 in Alabama. She died on 09 Jan
1976 in Harris county, Texas. She married **WADE L. JONES**. He was born about
1908 in Texas. He died on 03 Jan 1998 in Harris County, Texas.

v.   **HAZEL ENZOR** was born on 28 Jul 1915 in Enterprise, Alabama. She died on 28 Jul

1915 in Enterprise, Alabama.

More About Hazel Enzor:
Burial: Enterprise City Cemetery, Enterprise, Alabama

vi.   NELL JEAN ENZOR was born on 19 Sep 1917 in Alabama. She died on 13 Nov 1958 in Florida. She married FRED HOUSTON HUNT. He was born on 20 Oct 1903 in Florida. He died on 30 May 1988 in DeFuniak Springs, Florida.

More About Nell Jean Enzor:
Burial: Euchee Valley Cemetery, Walton County, Florida

40.   LOUISA JAMES[3] EDWARDS (Walter Starr[2], Ambrose[1]) was born on 10 Dec 1880 in Alabama. She died on 17 Jul 1953 in Greenville, Alabama. She married Nat Woodruff Thornton on 20 Apr 1900 in Coffee County, Alabama. He was born on 23 Jun 1873 in Barbour County, Alabama. He died on 30 Dec 1947 in Dothan, Alabama.

More About Nat Woodruff Thornton:
Living In: 1910 Enterprise, Alabama
Living In: 1920 Geneva, Geneva County, Alabama
Occupation: 1930 in Geneva, Geneva County, Alabama; Clerk of Probate Court

Nat Woodruff Thornton and Louisa James Edwards had the following children:

i.   JAMES WOODRUFF[4] THORNTON was born on 05 Feb 1901 in Enterprise, Alabama. He died in Sep 1972 in Montgomery, Alabama. He married MYRA KENDALL. She died after 1989.

ii.   SARAH NATALIE THORNTON was born on 20 Nov 1902. She married ROBERT DIXON BROWN.

iii. JONATHAN STARR THORNTON was born on 05 Feb 1905 in Enterprise, Alabama. He died on 24 Jan 1966 in Ashville, Alabama. He married MARGARET BROWN.

iv.   EDWARDS GREY THORNTON was born on 16 Mar 1910. He married MARGARERT LEWIS.

41.   CHARLES BROWN[3] EDWARDS (Walter Starr[2], Ambrose[1]) was born on 01 Apr 1884 in Enterprise, Alabama. He died on 28 Jun 1956 in Houston, Texas. He married EMILY EULALIA RIGDEN. She was born on 15 Aug 1889 in Geneva, Alabama. She died on 04 Oct 1970 in Houston, Texas.

More About Charles Brown Edwards:
Burial: 30 Jun 1956 in South Park Cemetery, Pearland, Brazoria County, Texas
Cause Of Death: Cerebral Hemorrhage
Living In: 1942 Galveston, Texas
Occupation: 1910 in Enterprise, Alabama; Rural Route Mail Carrier
Occupation: 1918 in Enterprise, Alabama; Rural Route Mail Carrier
Occupation: 1920 in Houston, Texas; Laborer at Automobile Company
Occupation: 1930 in Houston, Texas; Insurance Agent for Insurance Company
Occupation: 1940 in Houston, Texas; General Insurance Salesman
Occupation: U.S. Postal Service

More About Emily Eulalia Rigden:

Burial: 05 Oct 1970 in South Park Cemetery, Pearland, Brazoria County, Texas Cause Of Death: Generalized Arteriosclerosis

Charles Brown Edwards and Emily Eulalia Rigden had the following children:

    i.   SARAH GLADYS[4] EDWARDS was born about 1906 in Alabama. She married (UNKNOWN) SMITH.

        More About Sarah Gladys Edwards:
Living In: 1930 Sarah is divorced and with her son is living with her parents in Houston, Texas.
Living In: 1940 Sarah is divorced and, with her son, is living with her parents in Houston, Texas.
Occupation: 1930 in Houston, Texas; Stenographer at Storage House
Occupation: 1940 in Houston, Texas; Stenographer for File Manufacturer

    ii.   MAUD MAXINE EDWARDS was born about 1909.

    iii.   JULIUS EDWARDS was born about 1911.

        More About Julius Edwards:
Occupation: 1930 in Houston, Texas; Ice Company Platform Man

    iv.   CHARLES GLENN EDWARDS was born on 10 Mar 1913 in Enterprise, Alabama. He died on 10 May 1975 in Houston, Texas. He married LYLE GREYCOURT.

        More About Charles Glenn Edwards:
Burial: 12 May 1975 in South Memorial Park Cemetery, Pearland, Texas
Cause Of Death: Acute Myelomonocytic Leukemia
Occupation: 1930 in Houston, Texas; Messenger Boy for Railroad
Occupation: Salesman

    v.   WARREN EDWARDS was born about 1917.

42.   MACKEY MAUDE[3] EDWARDS (Walter Starr[2], Ambrose[1]) was born on 12 Jun 1887 in Alabama. She died on 23 Oct 1977 in Milton, Florida. She married WILLIAM BURIAN KILLEBREW. He was born on 18 Sep 1870 in Newton, Alabama. He died on 19 Nov 1946 in Galveston, Texas.

More About Mackey Maude Edwards:
Living In: 1900 Enterprise, Alabama
Living In: 1910 Hartford, Alabama
Occupation: 1920 in Angleton, Brazoria County, Texas; Public School Teacher
Occupation: 1930 in Jefferson County, Texas; Public School Teacher

Notes for Mackey Maude Edwards:
Mackey Maude Killebrew is name used on Social Security death index and Florida State death index.

More About William Burian Killebrew:
Cause Of Death: Bronchopneumonia
Occupation: 1900 in Newton, Dale County, Alabama; School Teacher
Occupation: 1910 in Hartford, Geneva County, Alabama; Teacher at State School

Occupation: 1920 in Angleton, Brazoria County, Texas; Public School Teacher
Occupation: 1930 in Jefferson County, Texas; Public School Teacher
Occupation: 1940 in Brazoria County, Texas; Retired

William Burian Killebrew and Mackey Maude Edwards had the following children:

i.   WILLIAM BURIAN[4] KILLEBREW was born about 1906 in Alabama.

ii. KATHERINE KILLEBREW was born on 17 Aug 1908 in Alabama. She died in May 1982 in Milton, Florida. She married DWIGHT LYMAN MIXON. He was born on 30 May 1899 in Coffee County, Alabama. He died in Dec 1973 in Milton, Florida.

43. LOVELACE YOUNG[3] EDWARDS (Walter Starr[2], Ambrose[1]) was born on 01 May 1889 in Enterprise, Alabama. He died on 15 Oct 1952 in Houston, Texas. He married Clara Inez Ralston, daughter of Wilbur L. Ralston and Barbara Frances Wampler on 16 Oct 1918 in Glendale, Arizona. She was born on 15 Oct 1891 in Dalton, Wayne County, Ohio. She died on 25 Dec 1976 in Houston, Texas.

More About Lovelace Young Edwards:
Burial: 16 Oct 1952 in Forest Park Cemetery, Houston,
Texas
Cause Of Death: Cerebral Hemorrhage, Arteriosclerosis
Living In: 1942 Houston, Texas
Occupation: 1917 in Glendale, Arizona; Book Keeper, Glendale Ice
Company
Occupation: 1920 in Phoenix, Arizona; Book Keeeper for Electric Company
Occupation: 1930 in Houston, Texas; Grocery Store Keeper
Occupation: 1940 in Houston, Texas; Partners in a cafe with his wife.

More About Clara Inez Ralston:
Burial: 27 Dec 1976 in Forest Park Cemetery, Houston, Texas
Occupation: 1930 in Houston, Texas; Clerk in Grocery Store
Occupation: 1940 in Houston, Texas; Partners in a cafe with her husband.

Lovelace Young Edwards and Clara Inez Ralston had the following child:

i.   BETTY[4] EDWARDS was born about 1923 in Arizona.

44. JOHNNIE EUDORA[3] EDWARDS (Walter Starr[2], Ambrose[1]) was born on 24 Feb 1892 in Enterprise, Alabama. She died in 1975 in Montgomery, Alabama. She married Angus Edwin Edwards, son of Robert Charles Edwards and Francesca La Coates on 20 Nov 1917 in Enterprise, Alabama. He was born on 07 Aug 1887 in Haw Ridge, Alabama. He died on 19 Mar 1966 in Montgomery, Alabama.

More About Angus Edwin Edwards:
Burial: Memorial Gardens, Montgomery, Alabama
Occupation: 1910 in Enterprise, Alabama; Laborer in Railroad Shop
Occupation: 1917 in Waycross, Georgia; Foreman on Railroad
Occupation: 1920 in Montgomery, Alabama; Machinist on Railroad
Occupation: 1930 in Montgomery, Alabama; Works in Railroad Roundhouse
Occupation: 1940 in Montgomery, Alabama; Locomotive Department Foreman on Railroad

Angus Edwin Edwards and Johnnie Eudora Edwards had the following children:

i.   HELEN FRANCES[4] EDWARDS was born on 20 Sep 1918 in Montgomery, Alabama. She died on 31 May 2002. She married Clyde Randall Holstead in 1939. He was born on 06 Jan 1915 in Ruston, Louisiana. He died on 19 May 1979.

ii. MARY CECIL EDWARDS was born on 09 Mar 1923 in Montgomery, Alabama. She married Phil Thurman Dunning II, son of Phil Thurman Dunning Sr. on 10 Oct 1941 in Montgomery, Alabama. He was born on 14 Jan 1920 in Hattiesburg, Mississippi. He died in Jan 2004.

9 781981 241149